Advance Praise for

Romancing the Web:
A Therapist's Guide to the Finer Points of Online Dating

"This in ... king for companio ... ive, safe and heal ... one who is searchi ...

--**Robert A. Dickens, Psychiatrist**

"This book is exactly what the internet dating community needed. It is a step by step analysis of what people need to do to prepare to enter the maze of the internet dating scene. It is a must read for anyone interested in internet dating, as well as for parents who may have young adult children interested in using this service."

--**Debra R. Mancoske, Attorney**

Romancing

the **WEB** ~

A Therapist's Guide to
the Finer Points of Online Dating

Diane M. Berry,
MSW, LCSW, JD

First Edition
Blue Waters Publications,
Manitowoc, Wisconsin

Romancing the Web
A Therapist's Guide to the Finer Points of Online Dating

© 2005 by Diane M. Berry, MSW, LCSW, JD

Blue Waters Publications, LLC
P. O. Box 411
Manitowoc, WI 54221-0411
Email: bluewaterspublications@lakefield.net
Website: www.bluewaterspublications.com

While the case studies and examples described in this book are based on interviews and situations experienced by real persons, the names, professions, locations and other biographical details have been changed to preserve their privacy and anonymity. Unless otherwise noted, examples provided in the text do not reflect actual persons, living or dead. Any resemblance to actual persons is purely coincidental.

Printed in the United States of America
ISBN, print ed.
ISBN, PDF ed.
First Printing 2005

Cover Design by Dunn+Associates

Publisher's Cataloging-in-Publication
(Provided by Quality Books, Inc.)

Berry, Diane M.
   Romancing the Web: a therapist's guide to the finer points of online dating / Diane M. Berry.--1st ed.
   p. cm.
   Includes bibliographical references and index.
   LCCN 2004117373
   ISBN 0-9742078-8-8

   1. Online dating   I. Title.

HQ801.82B47 2005   646.7'7'02854678
                         QBI04-200535

Dedication

This book is dedicated to my husband, Terry, my greatest supporter and my dearest friend. Witnessing the pain and heartache experienced by my clients and friends, I am continually reminded of the truly wonderful man I have been lucky enough to marry. Know that you are cherished and appreciated.

"Avoiding danger is no safer in the long run than outright exposure. Life is either a daring adventure or nothing."

~Helen Keller

.

Contents

Foreward

As an attorney dealing primarily with Family Law, I have come in contact with many cases in which online dating has caused torment and heartbreak for families. I have seen parents dating online, divorcing and abandoning their children, as well as singles being hurt or taken advantage of when unaware of some of the indicators of a destructive or predatory relationship. I have also seen kids go online unsupervised and meet older predator males desiring to do them harm.

This book is exactly what the internet dating community needed. It is a step by step analysis of what people need to do to prepare to enter the maze of the internet dating scene. It is a must read for anyone interested in internet dating. It is also an excellent resource for parents who may have young children interested in using this service.

Now, for the first time, a relationship therapist shows you how to write a profile to attract a healthy and positive relationship and how to read the profile of a potential partner to look for signs of trouble. This easily read volume will also help you to make appropriate choices about dating behaviors, both to advance and enhance the relationship, as well as to protect yourself and your family. You owe it to yourself to use this information to your best advantage!

Debra R. Mancoske,
Attorney at Law

Preface

A Note to the Reader

Whether you are picking up this book because you are already involved in online dating and looking for a few pointers or because it seems terrifying to even think about becoming involved in this phenomenon, you will find help here. Take your time, read through the chapters, paying particular attention to the examples provided and before long, you will be meeting new partners easily online.

Know, too, that you are part of the latest dating revolution. For a variety of reasons, online matchmaking is fast becoming the number one way couples connect. While a bit of common sense is required and traditional relationship skills and safety rules still apply, online dating is truly the way of the new millennium.

While there is not enough room in one volume to cover everything you need to know about dating online, I have attempted to give you a basic understanding of the mechanics of this process and a framework from which to begin. I encourage you to take the information contained herein and experiment with it. Jump right in and get your feet wet. Don't agonize about it or spend a lot of time contemplating the journey on which you are about to embark. Some of the most important lessons you will learn by experience; some may be painful, others will delight you. The important thing is just to get started.

If you are willing to share your insights and experiences, I would be honored to hear about them. Please email me at the address contained in the back of this book and your story may appear in the next edition.

Above all, use the information contained in this book to enjoy yourself! That's why you're interested in online dating, after all: to have fun and establish a fulfilling relationship!

Be smart, be safe and be happy. And enjoy your adventure!

Diane M. Berry
Manitowoc, Wisconsin

About the Author

Starting her professional career as a divorce attorney in 1983, Diane Berry quickly realized that she enjoyed dealing with the emotional aspects of a breakup more than the legal ones and headed back to school for her Master's Degree in Social Work. In 1995, Berry completed her schooling and began working as a therapist with clients struggling with the issues of depression, anxiety, stress management and life change adjustments. Divorce and step family adjustment became areas of specialty for her as she was able to combine her experience in the areas of law and social work.

As a result of her involvement with clients experiencing divorce and its aftermath, Berry became involved with a number of persons experimenting with online dating. After observing this phenomenon for a period of time, witnessing both mistakes and bouts of incredible wisdom amid pain, Berry felt compelled to offer some common sense suggestions for online singles. In her own words, Berry says, "When I started to feel like a parrot, repeating the same suggestions and ideas over and over again, to one client after another, I knew the time had come to write another book!" *Romancing the Web* is the product of that experience.

Berry also developed a four hour educational workshop, entitled Parenting Through Divorce, which became the basis for her first book, *Child-Friendly Divorce: A Divorce(d) Therapist's Guide to Helping Your Children Thrive*, published in March, 2004. Both the book and class explore the effects of divorce on children, discuss what parents can do to make things easier for their children and themselves, custody and placement arrangements for kids of all ages and outline how parents can restructure their relationship with each other, from one of intimate partners to one of business associates engaged in the task of cooperatively raising their children.

Berry has been interviewed for radio, television and newspaper reports on the class and has made presentations about the class to the local Bar Association and other community groups.

In addition to practicing therapy and teaching the Parenting Through Divorce Program, Berry also co-facilitates an Anger Management Group for men who have been arrested for domestic violence offenses, offers a six week divorce adjustment therapy group for adults experiencing divorce, as well as a Secrets of Successful Step Families Group for couples making that adjustment. Several times a year Berry offers free seminars to the public that she has designed and written on various stress management issues, and upon which the *Positively Managing Your Stress!* and *Soothing the Self* articles are based.

In May of 2000, Berry opened a small mental health clinic with her husband and another colleague. Acting as Director of the clinic, Berry continues her therapy practice, in addition to offering the Parenting Through Divorce and other groups mentioned above.

Following the publication of *Romancing the Web*, Berry has plans for works on adjusting to divorce, anger management and making a successful transition to step family life.

A Note on Gender

To avoid long and awkward phrasing within sentences, the publisher has chosen to randomly alternate the use of male and female pronouns in referring to individuals within this work to give acknowledgment to persons of both genders.

Acknowledgments

I have not attempted to cite in this volume all of the authorities and sources consulted in the preparation of this material. To do so would require more space than is available. This list would include government agencies, libraries, periodicals, Web sources and many individuals.

Scores of people contributed to this text, including many of my favorite clients who have braved the new frontier of dating and pursued online adventures, educating me in the process. You know who you are, but to the hundreds of individuals who have helped to educate me over the years about the intricacies of online dating, I offer these words: you are a courageous and generous breed, to not only embark on new adventures in an uncommon way, but to share your findings, your hopes, joys, triumphs and tribulations with millions of others seeking the same — a life partner. I salute you! This book is as much your work as it is mine!

Special thanks also go to Dr. Robert A. Dickens and Attorney Debra Mancoske for their kind words about this work. Thank you to Hobie and Kathi of Dunn+Design for another terrific cover in "love" but "non-girly" colors, to Dan Poynter for his continued wisdom and inspiration, and to my friend and right hand, Lisa Klein, for *all* she did to make this book possible. Believe me, I *do know* how much that was! You are truly a miracle worker!

I would like to express a final and heart-felt thanks to my family, who always seemed to understand when "Mom is writing." Your support means more than you know. This is my mission, but you are my inspiration. I am honored to have you in my life.

Disclaimer

This book is designed to provide information about the subject matter covered. It is sold with the understanding that the publisher and author are not engaged in rendering legal, accounting, therapy or other professional services. If legal, therapeutic or other expert assistance is required, the services of a competent professional should be sought.

It is not the purpose of this manual to reprint all the information that is otherwise available to persons on this subject matter, but to complement, amplify and supplement other texts. For more information, please see the many references in the Appendices.

Every effort has been made to make this book as complete and accurate as possible. However, it may contain mistakes, both typographical and in content. Therefore, this text should only be used as a general guide and not as the ultimate source of dating information. Further, this manual contains information on computer dating that is current only up to the printing date.

The purpose of this manual is to educate, inform and entertain. The author and Blue Waters Publications shall have neither liability nor responsibility to any person or entity with respect to any loss or damage caused or alleged to be caused directly or indirectly by the information contained in this book.

If you do not wish to be bound by the above disclaimer, you may return this book to the publisher for a full refund.

"A ship in harbour is safe,
but that is not what ships are built for."

~William Shedd

Introduction

Romance on the Web

Why a Book About Online Dating?

"**B**ut I just don't know where to start! I haven't dated in 20 years. I always thought I'd be married forever. And I never even used the computer!" Dave whined a bit as I made the suggestion that he attempt to meet someone on the computer.

"Don't worry Dave, it's like riding a bicycle," I reassure him, "It will all come back to you."

"I just don't know. I was never very good at dating. And where do I start with this computer thing anyway?"

This conversation is a common occurrence in my office. I am a therapist by profession and I work with many persons who experience divorce or the end of other long term relationships. When this happens, most of my clients struggle to adjust to the loss and then eventually look to find another partner.

To enable you to better understand their predicament, I must first set the stage. We live in a small Midwestern city with a population just short of 35,000 people. We tend to be a very married community and many of us who are not coupled up legally, are at least involved in serious long-term relationships. The reality is, it is very difficult to meet someone in the city in which I live and work. The population base is small; the singles' community is but a fraction of that and, due to the size of the community, there is not a wide variety of places to meet other single persons. Believe me, I have tried to find viable alternatives and I have given advice and made suggestions until I am blue in the face.

I have learned much from my clients over the years. One of my most important lessons is that, for a variety of reasons, most of the other viable options for meeting other singles are unworkable.   We will explore this further in Chapter One when we look at some of the societal changes that have made some former alternatives ineffective, but, for a quick overview, three of the most typical places people look for a new partner, churches, singles' bars and the workplace, are all problematic for various reasons.

Typically the churches have either an elderly or a married-with-children population so as a dating resource, they fall short. Most of the persons involved in the volunteer and political organizations are also married or otherwise unavailable.

Hanging around in bars or taverns to meet new people is not a healthy or viable alternative either. Even if you have the time, the desire and the patience to do this, you have to question the values and veracity of someone you meet while in a bar consuming alcohol. Even if you get "lucky" and do meet Mr. or Ms. Right, you run the risk of moving too fast or making inappropriate judgments. Many singles find that this activity simply becomes a waste of time which leads to poor judgment and damaged relationships.

In the past, many persons would meet their future partners at work. The practice of dating a co-worker can lead to a whole host of problems in and of itself; everything from discomfort at work if the relationship doesn't work out to violation of a company policy if your employer has rules against fraternization, which more and more companies are instituting. For these reasons, employment as a resource for romantic partners is typically problematic as well.

What's a healthy, well-adjusted single person to do?

When I suggest to my clients that they look to the computer to play cupid, many are incredulous. However, I have been working with clients for a number of years who have been intelligently and thoughtfully meeting and dating persons online for some time. It is a respectable and, if done correctly, safe method of meeting like-minded singles in your area and can provide a much wider population of potential partners from which to choose. In short, the computer can greatly increase your chances of finding that fulfilling relationship we all seek.

In my practice, I see between 20 and 25 individual clients each week, in addition to the groups and classes I do. In at least one half of those sessions, computer dating is discussed. I find myself saying the same things and making the same suggestions, over and over again. When I begin to feel like a parrot, I know the time has come to write a book which will help me reach a still wider audience.

My clients are certainly not the only ones with these questions or needing some basic information on this subject. I, therefore, write this book to share these general, common sense computer dating principles with all that will listen or read them. My aim is twofold: 1) to increase the number of singles finding satisfying long-term relationships and 2) to increase the safety of all those participating.

I look forward to hearing from readers who have followed the ideas espoused in this work, either in the interest of fine-tuning or "tweaking" the advice included herein, or to hear yet another success story from you. As you may surmise, many of the ideas I pass along in this book have come from clients and singles just like yourselves who have consented to allow me to use their stories to help someone else. If you are willing, please refer to Appendix B for the address to contact me and share your story. You may very well appear in the next edition.

As I have done in previous books I have written, each chapter begins with an example similar to an actual session I have had with a client that illustrates the principle espoused in that chapter. I believe it is easier to understand each concept with an example to which it applies. Each chapter, with the exception of the Introduction and Conclusion, also concludes with a summary page, which is designed to enable you to quickly review the key principles discussed in the chapter.

Please **do** take the time to read over these summaries and to review any sections of the chapter that are unclear to you, to increase your understanding of the concepts presented. This is not rocket science, but it can be confusing, especially if you are unfamiliar with the ideas being discussed. As with any new concepts we learn, it can be helpful to read about them more than once before attempting to act on them. Take the time to really think about and digest the material presented in each chapter before moving onto the next, as the information presented in following chapters builds on ideas previously discussed.

Good luck and enjoy! Even though taking risks and meeting new challenges can be frightening, it can also lead to great adventure! Make the most of it!

"There is as much risk in doing nothing,
as in doing something."

~Trammell Crow

Chapter 1

You're <u>Not</u> Desperate and You Don't Need Your Kids' Permission!

Why Computer Dating Has Become Acceptable

Mary sniffles tearfully in my office, clutching the tissue tightly to her cheek.

"She just doesn't understand how lonely I am for a companion. All she says is that I'm putting us all in danger and that she doesn't approve of what I'm doing. I feel so guilty and so desperate. Am I doing something wrong?"

"Not at all," I reassure her, *"Tell her it is perfectly acceptable to meet people online if you're careful how you do it. It's now become one of the primary ways of meeting people in this country."*

"I told her that and she says she doesn't care if you say it's OK; she just says it's dangerous!" she wails.

I had an actual session just like this one last week which was one of the final straws that pushed me into writing this book. I had been working on a manuscript on anger management, which is about half completed, but there seems to be much misinformation and confusion out there regarding computer dating and a real need for some guiding principles on how to do it.

In addition, there are a number of negative, destructive emotions associated with being in a situation where online dating seems an appealing alternative. Just considering this option can lead to feelings of shame, guilt and desperation. I am here to try to dispel these emotions. They are unjustified and damaging to the good people who are finding themselves in the situation to consider or explore online dating in an attempt to meet a companion or a life partner, whether they live in my small Wisconsin city or anywhere else.

I want to help potential daters, as well as their families and friends who try to dissuade them from exploring this option, to understand that there are some very real reasons that online dating makes sense. We have experienced a number of events in our evolution as a society that have eliminated a number of options we previously used to meet a life partner.

As we have evolved, we have placed ourselves in a situation which can be limiting and isolating in terms of finding companionship. As the door to former alternatives closes, the need is created for new options. In my opinion, one of the most healthy and appealing is online dating. Let's take a look at why this is the case.

Historical Significance

From a sociological perspective, there are several events in our past that set us up to believe that computer dating is an act of desperation. This sets the stage for some real difficulties in convincing many average Americans to give it a try. The problem then becomes that there are fewer potential partners for those more adventurous souls who conquer their fear of trying something new or unconventional. So let's spend a few minutes looking at what can get in the way of reaching out in this manner.

Dating services have been around for a number of years. When they were first developed, in the mid 1960's, our society was just beginning to change from one in which it was not uncommon for an individual to spend his entire life in the same town or city, if not the same house or homestead, into one considerably more mobile. The dating services were a reaction to the difficulty of meeting new, suitable partners in an unfamiliar setting, but they never seemed to gain the acceptance of the majority of the population. Rather, they were seen as an act of desperation by those undesirables who were unable to find a partner through the two more acceptable methods: being introduced through mutual friends or meeting someone at work.

Additionally, it is often difficult to accept new ideas as respectable. Think back to the reactions we hear about when the ideas of women wearing pants or being allowed to vote were first being bandied about. Many people, both male and female, were horrified to think of either eventuality coming to pass, or saw the ideas as so incredulous they were laughable. Today, thinking of these ideas as unacceptable seems incredible to most of us.

Because of the connection to these services and this early reaction to them, it is often assumed that anyone resorting to a computer to locate a match is either so undesirable that friends are reluctant to introduce them to other singles and/or co-workers who have a chance to get to know them will have no desire to make them a partner. This is unfortunate and completely inaccurate, as a new set of historical circumstances have led to the development, necessity and prevalence of computer dating.

Continued Change

As our society continued to change, several events occurred which resulted in increasing difficulty in meeting partners as our parents once did. First of all, we have become increasingly mobile, many of us changing cities every few years as we change jobs or positions within a company. We find ourselves losing contact with long term friends and have less time to even establish the new friendships we may form.

It also becomes more difficult to meet the good friends and make the connections with people who would know us well enough to introduce us to an acquaintance who might be a good partner. Many of these newer acquaintances are also either reluctant or inadequate matchmakers, either not wanting to get involved or choosing someone entirely inadequate for us due to a lack of information or being a poor judge of complementary qualities.

Secondly, many of us are working longer hours, which, again, cuts into the time we have available for meeting new people. Further, the time we do have is often late in the evening which is not necessarily conducive to making new contacts. We thus become more isolated and alone.

Third, extended family, which was formerly an important resource for meeting a potential life mate, as in the form of "my big brother's best friend from high school" or "my sister's roommate" and the like, is often scattered far and wide. Due to employment obligations, our contact with them is further limited, both in terms of frequency and duration, so we typically lose family as a resource in finding a partner.

Finally, people are living much longer than they used to and divorce is more prevalent, creating an even larger pool of persons who are not able to meet their life partners in high school or college. If we are divorced or widowed at an early age, we could have another fifty or sixty years of our life left. Do you really want to spend it alone? Most of us would answer with a resounding "No!"

Work as a Resource

In more recent times, once we became more mobile, many partners would find themselves meeting at the workplace. This is a resource that has worked for many couples and can still be effective. There are a couple of factors that limit its usefulness in all cases, however.

First of all, some employers have policies that directly prohibit this type of fraternization among employees. Even if that is not the case, if one member of the couple is the other's superior, trouble and discomfort is often the result, and there is a great potential for sexual harassment complaints. Additionally, some persons are extremely uncomfortable dating a co-worker because of the potential for disaster if the relationship ends. You should be extremely hesitant to embark on this type of a relationship if you cannot be relatively certain that you would both be able to continue with your current employment in the event the relationship ended.

Secondly, with the mobility factor, and due to many employers down-sizing or laying off on a regular basis, often there is not the longevity associated with a work situation for an intimate relationship to develop. Many co-workers simply do not have enough time together before some major change occurs on the job scene and they are abruptly parted.

Thirdly, exactly the opposite problem can occur. With the scarcity of good jobs in this day and age, many employees are staying at long-term jobs, rather than risking a new and unpredictable venture, especially when they are getting into their 40's and 50's. This can lead to a stagnant pool of potential partners in the work environment, where individuals may work with the same persons for ten or twenty years and, after a while, have investigated the possibility of a relationship with every available person of potential interest. Soon there are no other persons available that they either have not dated or ruled out for a variety of reasons.

This is a common situation that I see in my practice. Mary has been an administrative assistant with a large employer in the city for ten years. Most of her co-workers are already married. The one who is not is neither interested in a partner, nor does he have anything in common with Mary.

Dave has been a woodworker in a factory for twenty years. He works primarily with men in his job. The women working in the office are either married or twenty years his junior.

Because of their situations, both Dave and Mary have begun exploring computer dating. Both are respectable singles in their late 40's who attend church regularly and never thought **they** would be caught dead looking for a partner on the computer. Both have exhausted all other resources and spent many lonely evenings before logging on to dating websites. While neither met their life partner in the first year they were dating online, each has met a number of suitable candidates for companionship and spent many pleasant days and evenings in the company of a partner met in this manner.

Other Resources

There are a number of other places people have traditionally, or perhaps sporadically, met, that are also not the good reliable resources we need in terms of connecting people. Two of the most common of these are singles' bars and churches.

Singles' bars are a dreadful place to meet people. Intuitively we can understand why this is, but let's explore this a bit more in depth. First of all, you have to hang out too long to meet Mr. or Ms. Right, increasing the risk of developing a serious alcohol problem.

Secondly, there are no guarantees that the person you meet will be honest, available or the right person, especially while under the influence of alcohol. Many of us have had at least one extremely negative experience, meeting someone in a bar that was not what they seemed or was a completely inappropriate partner. Persons met in a bar are often under the influence of alcohol or other drugs and may not be honest about who they are. Further, the substances involved can serve to reduce inhibitions that assist us in making healthy and appropriate choices, sometimes with life-changing consequences.

Thirdly, if you meet a new person while drinking alcohol, you run the risk of moving too fast or making inappropriate judgments, such as that to engage in sexual contact too quickly. This can not only damage the relationship, but also endanger your life if it is a decision you make hastily and without adequate preparation.

Meeting a partner in a bar has also begun to carry such a stigma that often, when I ask how couples have met and this is the case, they lower their voices before they admit to meeting in such a setting. Feeling this ashamed or uncomfortable can only affect the relationship negatively.

Additionally, with the new drunk driving laws and the new awareness of the damage alcohol can do to our bodies, as well as the new health consciousness as the baby boomer generation ages and must take better care of themselves in order to lead healthier and more active lives, the idea of spending time in a bar has become a whole lot less appealing. For one thing, unless you are engaged in a lively conversation, it can be just plain boring. For another, most of us are just too busy with things we want and have to do to spend much time sitting in a tavern. As a result, waiting for our true love to walk through the door of our corner bar is just not an effective way to meet someone. Even if we have the time, the desire and the patience, as we said before, hanging around a bar is a great way to develop an alcohol problem.

In the past, many persons have looked to churches or religious organizations as a resource for partnership. However, the mobility of our society has largely eliminated spending a lifetime belonging to the same home parish. Additionally, churches tend to vary a great deal in terms of how effective a resource they are.

One of the most common complaints I hear from my clients regarding meeting people through church is that everyone is already married. Young couples often join a church, either to have a place to marry or to have a child baptized. Hence they are not available partners. Another common complaint I hear from clients joining a parish looking for companionship is that many of their fellow church-goers are elderly. While this can be a good thing if you are an older single, I have yet to locate a parish in my community populated with a large number of single persons seeking partners.

Other resources we have used in the past are special interest groups or organizations, such as the Jaycees, the Lions, political groups, and the like. While occasionally this may connect us with our perfect mate, and can be effective in that we know we at least share certain interests or values due to our common participation in the group, many of the factors that have made the family and workplace ineffective as matchmaker have affected this resource as well. Increased mobility and less time to get to know each other and to socialize are two of the main difficulties.

Locale as a Factor

Where you live is as important as who you are these days in terms of locating a mate. Singles living in cities with large single populations, or with large populations in general, can have more success in locating other singles to date. While a larger city can lead to greater isolation and greater difficulty connecting with anyone, much less other singles, it can also offer a wider variety of resources designed just for singles making it easier to connect as well.

One of these is a relatively new phenomenon called "Speed Dating," whereby an equal number of men and women are registered for an evening of meeting other singles briefly to discover whether there is anyone in the group they want to spend more time with. Often each woman chooses and sits at a table while the men spend three or five minutes at each table making polite and introductory conversation with each registered woman. A horn often signals the end of the "date" and cues the men to move on to another table.

At the end of the evening, participants complete a "scorecard" indicating which, if any, of their dates they would be willing to see again. Then, approximately a week after the experience, the singles get a letter in the mail giving them information about how to contact persons whose names they checked who have also indicated a desire to get to know them better.

In talking with one of my clients about his experience with "Speed Dating" he stated, "It wasn't so much that I met the perfect person or learned what I was looking for in a partner, but I learned that evening what I did NOT want in a partner or a relationship." He indicated he found it a very useful experience for that reason, but, again, was not able to use that particular experience to meet "Ms. Right." In other words, the person he truly got to know better was himself!

As useful as it could be in finding a partner, speed dating is not something that will likely be found in a small town. There simply isn't the population base to pull it off. For this reason, larger cities may have some resources, such as speed dating and special singles' events, that small towns cannot offer in terms of matchmaking.

Additionally, many smaller towns tend to be very "coupled up", depending on the norms in the part of the state or country in which they are located. As I told you previously, I live in a city of approximately 34,000 people in northeastern Wisconsin. It tends to be quite a conservative area and many residents are either married or already involved in long term relationships. There are few resources for singles, either to meet other singles or simply to socialize without a partner. For this reason, computer dating has taken off quite significantly in my area, despite its conservative tendencies.

One problem this has led to, however, is parents being criticized by their children for meeting other singles online. The values of the community are expressed by the adult children of these lonely and frustrated singles, leading to dissention and conflict in families!

Quite the contrast is Taos, New Mexico. While it, also, is a small town, in fact at approximately 7000 persons it is quite a bit smaller than Manitowoc, Wisconsin, there are many opportunities available in Taos for singles to meet. There are lectures on a variety of interesting topics, dances and dance lessons, a wide variety of movies in addition to the typical first run choices, discussion groups, musical groups to see, all in addition to informal social gatherings that occur on both a planned and spontaneous basis at various clubs in the city.

There is a wonderful gathering spot known as the Adobe Bar, located in the Old Taos Inn, which is known as the "living room of Taos." Many nights each week entertainment is available, surrounded by a large variety of comfortable seating arrangements conducive to conversation and connection. What a wonderful resource for singles!

Larger cities such as New York and Chicago tend to have larger numbers of single persons and, of necessity, provide more resources for them. Even in mid-sized cities, such as Cleveland, Indianapolis and San Francisco, there are a number of opportunities to meet interesting people that are not found in smaller, more coupled communities such as Manitowoc and other cities of its size. If you are looking to meet others without going online, you may just need to do some research and re-locate to a community that does cater more to singles.

Because of the limited opportunities available in these smaller cities, singles have, of necessity, begun to rely on computer dating to meet potential partners. Isn't that preferable to reconciling themselves to spending the rest of their lives alone? As long as it is done safely with a good measure of common sense, computer dating can be a start of a wonderful relationship.

Advantages of Online Dating

There are also a number of distinct and definite advantages to dating online that I can think of, in addition to putting you in touch with a larger pool of prospects than staying within your home community as discussed above. For one thing, you have a great deal of control over the process. You choose your site, what you want to say, how involved you want to be, who you want to contact and when and how you want to contact them.

Further, you do have that wide selection of people to choose from, and they typically have their likes, dislikes, personality styles and what they are looking for listed right there in front of you. It's like a proverbial candy store full of potential life partners!

Additionally, distance is not necessarily a problem because you are not relying on face to face contact to begin your relationship. You can live in a town of 200 people and be separated from your prospects by several hundred or several thousand miles, and this needn't prevent you from at least investigating whether a relationship is worth pursuing. Because you will be spending much time getting to know people using the various technologies available to us, such as the computer, internet and telephones, your relationships can develop to a pretty substantial degree, even with the two of you living a significant distance apart.

Don't let distance get in your way. If the relationship works, the other details can often be worked out later. Some couples even make long distance relationships work long term, but that could be the subject of another entire book so I won't go into detail about that here.

Finally, and this is closely akin to the control aspect, you are in charge of the timing. You decide when to have this contact. Most people have many demands on their time: a full time job, a home to maintain, perhaps children to raise. Maybe the only time you have available to look for a social life is from 11:00 p.m. to midnight when all of your other obligations are settled for the day. You can date online at anytime of the day or night.

If you're up at 3:00 a.m. and want to check your email or change your profile, go for it. The therapist in me, however, is wondering why you are up at 3:00 a.m. Perhaps this is something we should talk about…

The bottom line is that there are a number of real advantages to dating online. These are just a few of the more significant ones. It has become the primary way singles are meeting these days, especially in smaller communities. And it has made great strides in the areas of respectability and acceptability to the general public. This means that the people you meet will likely be nice people just like yourself who are a bit lonely and in search of some companionship.

I have summarized the main points of this chapter on the following page. This can be a useful tool to read over to boost your confidence if you are attempting to work up the courage to complete your first profile or "wink" at your first possible candidate. It can also be helpful in preparing for a conversation with an adult child who is attempting to convince you that the only people who participate in online dating are immoral, desperate and dangerous.

It is important to stress, both to yourself and to others, the sociological factors and changes that have affected our lifestyles and families over the past 100 years. Looking at this information in historical perspective illustrates what a wonderful and timely resource computer dating can be.

*"One's mind, once stretched by a new idea,
never regains its original dimensions."*

~Oliver Wendell Holmes

"You're Not Desperate" Summary

♡ Computer Dating is a new idea whose time has come, much the same as the vote for women in the 1920's. Some people take longer to adjust to new ideas.

♡ Our society has changed in some significant ways that make the old ways of meeting other singles obsolete:
~increased mobility,
~longer work hours, and
~less contact with extended family and other potential resources.

♡ Work is not the resource it once was for a number of reasons:
~company policies against "fraternization",
~increasing mobility,
~an economy that keeps us stuck in the same work environment long after we have explored the potential partners there.

♡ Other resources are not healthy places to meet partners or do not have a pool of potential partners: singles' bars, churches, other organizations.

♡ If we live in a small or "coupled up" community that does not cater to or provide services for singles, we may have few resources available to meet people. Moving may be an option, but adult children may hold us to our home environment.

♡ There are some distinct advantages to online dating, such as the matters of:
~control   ~choice
~ease of long distance relationships   ~timing

♡ If done safely and with a healthy dose of common sense, computer dating can be a wonderful resource for meeting a life partner or a companion.

"If you're not willing to risk the unusual,
you will have to settle
for the ordinary."

~Jim Rohn

Chapter 2

A Site to Behold!

Some of the Best Websites for Meeting Other Singles

"I'm seeing a man named Michael who is a Lutheran Pastor down in Iowa," Sandra tells me in our first session together. She has already informed me how important her faith and church involvement are in her life.*

"That's quite a distance from here," I remark, "How did you two meet?"

"On a Lutheran dating website. I've met several other guys there, too, really nice men, but Michael and I really seem to hit it off. We both have a very strong faith, Christian values and similar goals in life. We feel lucky to have found each other."

There is a wide variety of websites to which you can go to meet your mate. In this chapter we will explore some of these sites and provide a little information about them, such as how to get there and what to expect. However, it would be a mistake to view this as an exhaustive list, for several reasons.

First of all, new sites are started almost daily. By the time this book hits the shelves, there will be many more sites than exist as I write this. Additionally, it is not important to learn every detail about sites you will never use. Therefore, I will attempt to provide some general information that should apply to most sites and give you some direction about various sites you may want to explore.

The other reason is that there is not enough room in a book like this to include a list of all available sites. There are simply too many options out there. What I attempt to do in this chapter is simply to give you an idea of some of the different ideas and options there are. Think of it as a starting point in your search. You may try one of the sites mentioned here and use that as a springboard for other similar sites. I am merely trying to give you an idea of the different places to look and to provide some options that may not occur to you independently. Happy searching!

Because each site is different in terms of profile format and questions, I will also not be providing specific details regarding the profiles of any particular site. What I will share with you is general information for completing or evaluating a profile as the information requested and sought is often quite similar, just listed or formatted a bit differently for each site. What you will need to do is generalize from the next few chapters to apply the information specifically to whichever site you are exploring.

As an aside, I would welcome, for future editions, any ideas or sites you stumble on that impress you that I have not included here. Please pass them on to me so I may share them with future readers. Also, while this is not meant to be a critique of dating websites, if there are any sites that you have had negative experiences with, please pass that information along to me as well, so I may include it in the next edition of this work, if it is appropriate.

The Leader of the Pack—www.match.com

While this is not to be interpreted as an endorsement of any kind, I will tell you that the website that I hear and see the most from my clients about is www.match.com. While this is not, by any means a scientific survey or result, in my practice, in my small town in northeastern Wisconsin, if my experience is any gauge, this is a popular starting point for computer dating. Even among my clients who explore other sites, most either start with or continue to be registered with match.com. As a result, this is the site with which I am most familiar.

I can tell you that, like many other sites, this one asks you to complete a series of multiple choice profile questions, then to write a statement at the end telling a little more about yourself. All of the suggestions included in the following chapter regarding completing your profile can be applied to the match.com questionnaire.

I will also share with you, as some of my clients have shared with me, that you can try the site at no charge for a brief period of time. However, while you can enter a profile, receive information and view profiles of singles that are available, I believe you must register and pay the fee to actually contact them. It would appear that the free trial is only to get an idea of and to "whet your appetite" for the singles available to you. While we can understand why they do this, this has led to some frustration on the part of persons trying out the site.

Another aspect to be aware of is that some participants learned after they had registered and paid their fee, that a number of the singles listed as available had not been active or online for a significant period of time. Some had been inactive for weeks or months. This, also, has led to some frustration and disappointment for potential partners.

But, generally, this can be a good starting point. Even my clients who start or end up at other sites typically have some contact with the "match" site. It is reportedly easy to understand and not difficult to get started. Additionally, the trial period can at least allow you to gather information about some potential contacts. For these reasons, you may want to start there.

Other General Dating Sites

There are a number of other general interest dating sites I have heard mentioned more than once by some of my favorite clients. A few of the most popular include:

♡www.datemate.com
♡www.singleme.com
♡www.eharmony.com
♡www.udate.com
♡www.kiss.com
♡www.americansingles.com
♡www.myematch.com
♡www.webdate.com
♡www.soulmatch.com
♡www.overthirtysingles.com
♡www.gay.com
♡www.friendfinder.com
♡www.epersonals.com
♡www.plentyoffish.com
♡www.usamatch.com

As I have heard less about these sites, I am also less familiar with their particular profiles than I am with that of www.match.com. Further, sites are changing rapidly and new sites are starting up on a daily basis. As a result, by the time this book is in print, any specific information I could give you would be outdated.

Accordingly, I have attempted to include general online dating principles regarding creating a profile, communicating and making relationship decisions that you will be able to apply, no matter which site you choose. My best advice is to use these general principles, but take the time to familiarize yourself with the specific rules and profiles of whichever site you use. Therefore, while there is less specific information I will offer you about some of these other sites, most of the information specific to www.match.com can be generalized and applied to any of the general dating sites you come in contact with.

Choosing Yourself vs. Allowing the Site to Choose for You

You should be aware that, while most sites allow you to peruse the profiles of online dates and make your choices about whom you want to contact, others will not permit you to do this. The latter type of site will take your responses to an extensive series of multiple choice questions, somewhat similar to a psychological test, such as the MMPI (Minnesota Multiphasic Personality Inventory), and will choose potential partners for you from among their pool of applicants that they determine are the best match for you.

One of the sites that operate in this manner is www.eharmony.com. While it can be helpful to have some choices made for you, some online daters are offended at being told who they are to choose from. If this approach suits you, you may want to check out this site. If you are turned off by this idea, you would probably be better off using another site. Again, check out the policies of any site you are thinking about working with to determine how matches are made.

Sites Catering to Special Interests

The possibilities in this category are almost too numerous to mention. Virtually any site on a subject of interest to you may have a dating component available. Whether the site you frequent caters to fans of particular sports teams, particular types of music, alumni of your high school or college or other special interests or needs, such as single parents or persons suffering from depression or anxiety, to give a couple of examples, check out the site to see if there is not some opportunity to meet other singles. Again, I will provide limited examples because the possibilities are endless. Just keep this idea in your mind as you are surfing the web.

To give you a general idea of what some of these sites may look like, if you are a fan of the Green Bay Packers, the NFL football team in my home state, you may want to "chat" with other "Packer fans" or join a fan club. You can connect with other fans by logging onto www.packers.com/fans/. You will have the opportunity to chat with other fans and will be given information about fan clubs available in different areas.

It is not designed specifically for meeting partners, but fans sharing a common enthusiasm for a team may find they have other interests in common as well.

If you are a single parent and looking for other singles with children, you may want to log on to www.singleparentmeet.com or www.singleparentsmingle.com. Both allow the opportunity to register free and post a greeting and a photo. The latter even gives visitors the opportunity for a live online chat with other single parents.

Virtually any area of interest to you may also give you the opportunity to connect with similarly interested singles online. While some of these sites do not have the safeguards those designed with dating in mind provide, they do have the added benefit of connecting persons interested in particular topics or subjects, rather than simply looking for a love connection.

Sites Connecting Singles with Similar Religious Beliefs

One option that few persons may realize exists, but one that may make many feel more comfortable about pursuing online relationships is that of faith-based dating sites. Several clients have met partners on sites such as these and have been reassured to know that they and their potential dates share similar values and beliefs.

The one drawback to these sites seems to be that, as they are drawing from a nationwide audience that is somewhat sporadically involved in online dating, matches can be with persons geographically distant from you. While it makes sense to check them out if this is a type of site that appeals to you, think carefully about whether or not you would be interested in a relationship with someone from a neighboring state or the other coast. After you are already involved it can be heart wrenching to have to make the choice to end the relationship because you are not up to the ten hour drive that separates you or find seeing each other once every three or four months insufficient.

To give you a couple of the more common examples of these types of sites, check out the following:

♡www.CatholicCupid.com
♡www.CatholicWeb.com: Singles
♡www.thrivent.com:LutheransOnline: SinglesSeeking
♡www.christiansingles.com
♡www.spiritualsingles.com

Catholic Cupid bills itself as "a great place for Catholics to build faith or seek happiness, hope, meaning or truth" and to interact with others. Restrictions include: no personal attacks against others, no foul language and no church-bashing. There is also an instant messaging and chat capability to have a brief conversation with potential partners. Registration is required to obtain information about others or to chat, but you are given the opportunity to place a free ad online which is said to take less than a minute to complete.

The other Catholic site I am familiar with is a part of www.CatholicWeb.com. If you log on to this general site, then select "Singles" at the top of the page, you have the opportunity to join at no charge and complete a profile. You may also obtain a preview of members online, which provides a few sentences about each person, but to access the actual profile of an individual or to contact them, you must register and join. The site indicates that certain important pieces of information, such as a registrant's last name, address, phone and email address will be kept confidential from other members.

Both of these sites list terms of use, to which users must agree before being able to proceed. Terms involve types of conduct and use of the information obtained about other members. Both sites contain stern warnings about spammers accessing and using information obtained on the site.

The Lutheran site I am aware of is accessed via the site www.thrivent.com and choosing "Lutherans Online" when given the opportunity and clicking on "Singles Seeking." Participants are able to do what is called a "Quick Search" to determine, for instance, if there are any 40-50 year old men in their state seeking partners, but to actually respond to a member profile, they must register on the site. There is also a message board and a chat room, which includes messages from participants to which registrants may also respond. These are just several examples of the types of sites available out there to find someone with shared values and beliefs. To find a site for members of your religious affiliation, or to determine what is out there, simply do a search for general websites regarding your faith and go from there. You should be able to get to some options for dating or seeking other like-minded singles.

Chat Rooms

A number of websites have chat room components that provide the opportunity for willing persons to meet each other, even if that is not their intended purpose. For example, the Oprah.com website has an online support group for those desiring to quit smoking and another for those attempting to lose weight. While there may be a primarily female viewership for the Oprah show, I know from my practice there are a significant number of men who do watch the show and read her magazine.

In our waiting room, *Oprah* is one of the magazines we have available for clients to read while waiting for appointments. As many as one third to one half of my male clients can be found reading the *Oprah* magazines in our lobby. They are interested and intrigued; they just may not want women to know that at all times. I can only assume there are a number of them online as well. While these online support groups are designed for those attempting to change problem behaviors, rather than to meet potential partners, due to the fact that persons are meeting and having contact with strangers, the can be a way to form a connection.

I offer this suggestion not as a primary source of dating relationships, but only to help you to "think outside the box" and see the opportunities presented to you in all of your interactions with other individuals. No matter where you are, there is the opportunity to meet the right person. You just need to stay open to it and to remain aware of those around you.

Because contact with these sites is not designed for meeting potential partners, but dealing with other issues, there are typically not the safeguards included that may be available on other sites. For this reason, you will want to be cautious about how much and how quickly to share specific, identifiable information about yourself with someone you meet in this manner.

Online Games

Another resource that is often overlooked by singles is the various online games that potential partners may play. Two common examples are "Everquest" and "The Realm" (www.everquest.com and www.therealm.com). I have several clients that have, somewhat unintentionally, connected with partners on this type of site, just by virtue of playing the game over a period of months or years.

While neither dating nor connecting with a partner is a primary focus of these sites, it often happens incidentally to regular contact in the course of playing the game. This happens quite naturally as, while in pursuit of the "crystal leaf" or some such treasure, players engage in conversation with teammates and partners and grow to know each other very well.

Long term relationships are often formed as a result of these contacts. In fact both of the clients I spoke of only developed the romantic interest after playing and knowing the partner on the game for in excess of six months! You can get to know a person very well with this much contact. This is especially likely because players of these games tend to be rather fanatical about it; most play every day or at least several times per week. That's a lot of contact!

An additional benefit of meeting a partner in this manner is that you know you share an interest in this type of computer game. This can be a quick way to connect, as long as the game does not begin to come between you once your "real life" relationship begins to develop (i.e., one of you wants to spend all your free time online as opposed to spending quality time with each other).

As an aside, I know relationships that have ended over games such as these as well. After all, a partner spending the majority of his free time online has little time or energy left to offer his own partner. Therefore, it would be wise to discuss moderation if this is an interest of yours.

Web Provider Sites

My web service provider has a number of other services available to its subscribers. For instance, there is a service called Cybertrader on which subscribers can list items for sale, free of charge. The list is available only to other subscribers of that service. Some web provider services have listings of singles seeking singles, similar to the listing of personal ads in the local newspaper.

Again, you want to be cautious about providing information about yourself in responding to one of these ads, as you typically do not have a complete profile or the safeguards typical to a dating site, but only a line or two about what type of person or relationship the individual is seeking. Be cautious in providing only limited information, such as a first name. I list this just as one more opportunity to meet other singles, not as an endorsement. Also, use this idea as an opportunity to think about which other potential service providers may also make this type of opportunity available.

Other Options

I want to stress that I offer these suggestions not as an exhaustive list, but only as a starting point for available sites to meet singles. Anyone reading this chapter can easily think of a number of sites they most likely frequent regularly that may have this option available. Often, we think of familiar sites only in terms of the business we regularly conduct there, not as having this potential. Take some time to think seriously about sites you are regularly visiting that may potentially lead to your contact with other singles.

Where to Start

Now that we have explored the wide variety of types of websites on which it is possible to meet a partner, where do you begin?

My recommendation, if you are new to online dating, is to go to one of the sites devoted to that purpose. You will have a number of safeguards in place to ensure your anonymity so that you are in control of how much information you want to share and with whom. In addition, the questionnaires and profiles provided can help walk you through the process of what and how to share information about yourself, in addition to giving you valuable information about a potential partner.

Also, you know others there are looking for contacts and companionship. If you connect through incidental contact on a game site, you have little idea if your potential partner is married or committed elsewhere or otherwise not truly interested in making a match.

If you do choose to make a connection with a potential partner on a non-dating site, in spite of my warnings, prepare yourself to do a bit of detective work on your own to ensure your safety. Whatever information you are able to gather about the individual can often be plugged into some type of an investigative website to give you more information or to validate what you are being told.

For example, in Wisconsin we have the ability to simply type an individual's name into a "Court Access" website and immediately learn about any court actions, civil or criminal, in which that individual, or someone with that name, is involved. This can tell you whether there is a divorce pending, whether he has been arrested for domestic violence or battery and many other useful things. Do not be afraid to make use of these tools that are made available by most state governments, free of charge. They can and will help to protect your safety if you use them wisely.

Learn About Your Site

No matter which site you use, whether you do go to an online dating site or investigate partners you have come to know through other incidental contact, take some time to learn about the site you are on. Especially if the site is new to you, spend some time on it; play with it to learn all of the options possible. It is often a good idea to do as much of this as you are allowed before you pay for a membership of any kind. Then, as soon as you become a paid member, you will be able to take advantage of all of the benefits available.

What you will be looking for when you are exploring is all of the options the site contains. Some provide a personality profile you may complete, aside from your own representations about your likes and dislikes, that you may have the ability to make available to potential matches. Often when this is completed, the site can provide a rating as to how appropriate a match you would be to any partner you are considering contacting or who may have contacted you. This can be useful information in terms of interests and compatibility.

Again, your focus here is to take advantage of all of the opportunities you are paying for. Your goal is to make as many matches as possible because online dating is, in many ways, a numbers game. While it only takes one match for happiness and companionship, the greater the number of available singles you can see and contact, the greater your likelihood of meeting just the right person. Spending time learning about these options before you pay can maximize the return on your investment.

One other issue you will want to research is the extent to which your site will be sharing information about you with other dating sites. There are a number of sites that will share your entire profile with other sites. While I do not know this firsthand, I am told by my clients that www.match.com is one of the dating sites that will do this, but by no means is it the only one. At one level or another, many of these dating sites are interconnected. To avoid being surprised by receiving a contact from an individual through a site with which you never registered, be sure to read the fine print in the Terms of Access section before you give your approval to it.

I have had clients that have been contacted by individuals not appearing on the site the clients had registered with, so they were unable to access a profile or learn more information than the individuals wanted to share. This puts you at a disadvantage in a game where knowledge is power and crucial for your safety. If you cannot tell, always ask a contact where she got your name or profile from and if she will not tell you, end your contact immediately. In each case that I am aware of, things ended badly for my clients as the persons contacting them were not who they were pretending to be. However, just knowing which sites your profile or information will be made available to can better prepare you for this kind of experience.

After you've given these issues some thought and perused the user history on your computer to determine if there are any sites you visit regularly that provide match-making possibilities, take a look at the summary on the following page. Again, it will help you think with an open mind about the opportunities and possibilities available to you.

Happy Hunting!

"It had long come to my attention
that people of accomplishment rarely sat back
and let things happen to them.
They went out and happened to things."

~Johann Goethe

"A Site to Behold!" Summary

♡   Investigate a number of sites before choosing one.

♡   Think about sites you visit regularly that may have a dating component.

♡   Don't overlook sites catering to various values and beliefs.

♡   Chat rooms devoted to other special interests (quitting smoking, losing weight) may be a way to connect with other singles.

♡   Online games may be a way to develop connections with others singles as well.

♡   Be aware that, when you meet someone on a site not exclusively devoted to online dating, you rarely have access to a profile or background information about the individual so you may have to do more detective work on your own.

♡   No matter which site you choose, familiarize yourself with all of the options and features particular to that site so you can take advantage of all you are paying for.

♡   Familiarize yourself with the "fine print", also, so you know whether your profile information will be shared with other individuals or sites so you are not surprised by a contact from an unfamiliar site.

Chapter 3

Once Upon a Time...

Completing Your Profile and Getting Started

"I *just don't know about this," Julie sighs in my office, "I don't know what to write."*

"Well, jot down some thoughts, some things you would like someone to know about you, and bring them along to your next session. We'll see if we can't put them together," I reassure her.

Julie breathes a sigh of relief, "Oh, that would be great! I just can't think where to start!"

The first point I want to make about this chapter and the above example is that these feelings are perfectly normal. In the first place, we are typically socialized to downplay our positive qualities. Comments such as, "Don't get a big head," "Don't blow your own horn," and "It's not polite to brag," are commonly heard, or at least understood while we are growing up. Now we are in a position where we are expected to do all of those things and for most of us this becomes extremely uncomfortable.

Secondly, we have grown up with the idea that responding to personal ads is an act of desperation. We can convince ourselves that computer dating is an acceptable way to meet other singles in this day and age, but the moment in time when we are most likely to experience a lack of confidence is when we come to complete our profile online. Just thinking of the information we want to put out there can give us the willies!

It is also normal to feel confused, uncertain and scared. We are complex persons with multiple components to our lives and our personalities. In attempting to think of a few sentences that will attract a person with similar interests and goals, what do we emphasize? How do we condense all of that information into 100 words or less? What should I say to attract a person I want to be with? Will I say the wrong thing or attract the wrong kind of person? Will I get hurt?

The best thing you can do to conquer some of these feelings and fears is to read on. There is nothing like a short course in marketing and relationship skills to boost your confidence again. At the end of this book, in Appendix C you will find a sample profile. In Appendices D and E, profiles of a different sort are included, one which raises red flags, the next with responses more akin to what you are looking for. Take a look at them. They, too, can give you some ideas of what you do and don't want to say.

If relationship skills have not been an area of strength for you in the past, in that a number of your previous relationships have ended badly, you may want to read this chapter over several times before moving on or posting online. For most of us, we often need to hear, read or learn new concepts several times before they truly sink in and become part of our awareness. Perhaps there are some things you need to work on in how you present yourself to others or how you approach relationships before you are ready to take on a new relationship.

Marketing, Marketing, Marketing

Just like the real estate slogan that states that the three most important qualities of any property are "Location, location, location", the most important thing about an online dating profile is marketing, marketing, marketing. When a company has a product to sell, it takes great pains to present it to the public in its best light so it will attract the greatest number of buyers. They are not being deceitful or dishonest, just pointing out the attributes of the product and what it can do for consumers. Think of your personal profile the same way.

You are attempting to attract a partner or partners. Give yourself some time to think about the following questions before writing or inputting your profile information.

♡What **positive qualities** do you have to offer a companion? Do you have a good sense of humor? Are you a caring person? Are you reliable, someone a person can count on? Are you fun to be with? What have friends and former partners told you about yourself (the good things)? Jot some of these down while you are thinking; then move on to the next question.

♡Think about the qualities someone else might be **looking for** in a partner. Some common characteristics might be someone who is faithful, loyal, empathic, caring, loving, fun to be with, a good listener, physically active and the like. No one will fit all of these characteristics, but do you fit some of them? Add them to your list.

Can you think of other qualities? Read over some of the profiles of potential partners. Jot down some of the things they say they are looking for. Do you fit any of these characteristics? Add them to your list. No one will fit all of them so don't expect that you will.

♡What do **you** want in a relationship? Are you looking to meet a number of people to just have fun and casual relationships with? Or are you looking for something more serious. Does the person you are looking have to love golf or cocker spaniels or be a practicing Catholic? If these types of things are very important to you, put them in your profile. Then you will be less likely to be disappointed. Add these qualities to your request or "Looking for" list.

You now have the meat of your ad. All that is left is to clean it up and make it a bit more presentable. For the remainder of this chapter, we will talk about how to do that. You should have things well thought out and your profile or ad prepared before you go to post your ad online. Before you log on, read on.

The Approach

There are several components that are important and should be considered in the work of making your list into a profile. This is the relationship skills portion of the chapter; these are effective ideas for presenting yourself to people you meet, whether in person or online. For our purposes, we will use examples to illustrate these points that are focused on creating the online profile. We will discuss each of these below, with some examples to help you use the ideas in making your own statement.

Be Clear

It is important to be clear about what you are looking for so that you are accurately understood. You can write the best, wittiest, most interesting profile in the world, but if it does not attract the type of partner or relationship you are looking for, it is not doing you any good. For example, if you are looking for a serious relationship, but emphasize qualities that scream "casual" and "fun" relationships with no commitment, your message will not be coming through clearly.

I would encourage you to put your pen down or remove your hands from the keyboard for a few minutes while you think seriously about the type of relationship you are seeking. Are you just seeking one or several companions to enjoy life and have some fun with? Are you looking for a platonic friend of the opposite sex because you always wanted a brother or sister to hang around with? Or, are you looking for a serious relationship that will eventually proceed to an exclusive and long term commitment if everything works out.

While each of these is an appropriate goal to seek from an online dating site, you want to make sure you know what you are looking for before you begin, so you are more likely to get it. Make sure your message is clear about what type of relationship you are seeking. Even if you are looking for a serious relationship, you always want to be careful not to put yourself in danger or scare people off by moving too quickly.

Take pains not to be evasive in the statements you are making. Share as much information as you are comfortable sharing in response to the questions asked, but do not resort to giving vague, avoidant answers if you are reluctant to state the whole truth. If you are uncomfortable giving personal information such as weight or income, say so openly in the manner suggested later in this chapter.

Clarity also goes to presentation. Don't use hard to read fonts, colors or all capital letters. People want to be interested and drawn in, not screamed at when you post a message. Simplicity is best.

Be Honest

Honesty is always the best policy, whether you are talking about the type of relationship you are seeking (don't say "just for fun" if you are looking for a serious partner—you **do** get what you ask for), your personal appearance, financial or employment issues or marital status. The truth always comes out eventually, especially if the relationship lasts. Dishonesty in your profile can do lasting damage to your relationship from which it can be difficult to recover. Don't take the chance of ruining the relationship before it even begins by being dishonest in your profile.

Avoid even minor deceptions in your online communications. If my clients are any gauge, and I tend to believe they are, online daters are a highly suspicious lot. They are aware of the dangers of online dating and know people can tell them anything and get away with it. Most daters that I know will simply disappear if they believe someone is lying or even being slightly deceptive with them. Don't take this chance. Be honest and make sure your profile, essays and follow-up emails are consistent.

One of my main techniques in assisting clients with online dating is helping them assess potential partners and relationships. I will typically ask clients to bring in the profile of contacts in which they are interested and to print out any emails they have written or received. I can pretty quickly assess whether the comments and information seem genuine and consistent or appear to be "put on" or fraudulent. People tend to give themselves away. They can attempt to come across a certain way, but will eventually get tripped up by their own words.

Honesty about yourself, even about potentially negative qualities, can lead to positive aspects of a new relationship. If you include in your profile that you are a bit chubby or have a few pounds to lose, you may attract a workout partner or someone who is interested in cooking and eating healthy meals. If you are tall and want to connect with a partner near your own height, say so. Remember, you **do** get what you ask for.

If money is an issue for you, honesty about this may attract a very frugal partner who can be helpful with budgeting or saving. Or who can help to share expenses by bartering services, such as car maintenance, laundry, lawn mowing or child care, to help you both out. Don't pretend you have the resources of Donald Trump or Oprah Winfrey if you can't back it up.

The internet is frequented by all kinds of people, just as the world is. You stand little chance of attracting the person you are looking for if you are not honest with yourself and in your profile about who that is. Don't sell yourself short or assume the person you are looking for won't be attracted by your qualities. You would be surprised at the number of very nice, honest, decent, respectable people who are dating online these days in search of companionship and more.

Be Positive

While we are being honest, we can still put the most positive "spin" on our characteristics. I realize the word "spin" has a rather negative connotation due to its unfortunate association with recent political campaigns, but it actually means nothing more than having a positive attitude. And isn't that a wonderful quality to find in a life partner?

Think of it this way: If you are in the midst of a crisis, who will you want to be spending time or sharing the experience with? The partner who bemoans, "This is awful; this is a nightmare!" or the one who can see the silver lining? I know who I'd choose.

I am not suggesting that you be deceitful here. The English language contains a number of adjectives that convey the same meaning. I am merely suggesting that you use the more positive adjectives in your profile. For example:

♡Use "Rubenesque" instead of "overweight"
♡Use "thrifty" or "frugal" instead of "cheap"
♡Use "mature" instead of "old"
♡Use "determined" instead of "stubborn"

For additional help, use the Thesaurus on your computer to search out positive adjectives for seemingly negative qualities.

These suggestions apply to your likes and dislikes as well. Indicating that you "can party without cocktails" is much more positive than "I hate drunks." No matter what you want to say, try turning it around and seeking to say what you do like, rather than what you dislike. This tends to help you find what you are looking for. You want to convey the sense that you are open to and willing to try new things.

After all, you might find a new hobby you would never have tried if not for a new relationship. One of my clients met a man online who loved to sail. She discovered it was a love of hers as well and, even though the relationship ended, she still has this new hobby to enjoy.

Be Respectful

Above all, the information you provide in your profile should be tasteful, sincere, respectful and courteous to all readers. Derogatory names, sarcasm, profanity (if the site even allows it) and overtly sexual references are to be avoided. Remember, using sarcasm and derogatory names will attract a certain type of person. Ask yourself if that is what you are looking for. Think carefully about your word choice in the statements you make. Know that what you write or infer about sex is going to determine, more than you can even imagine, how your prospects respond. Less is more.

An important point to keep in mind is that comments, whether it is sexual innuendo, frustration, anger or any other strong emotion, tend to come across much more strongly in an online profile or email than when you say them in person. This is because there is no eye contact, body language, gestures or tone of voice to assist in interpreting or softening the statements. All we have are the words themselves—which can speak pretty loudly in the absence of the other data we are accustomed to using to evaluate them.

Know that any comments or references to sex will typically be given the most sexually explicit interpretation possible. Know, too, that there are a series of words that refer to sex, without saying it explicitly, so think carefully about whether or not you want to include them in your profile. As a relationship therapist, I would recommend avoiding them until much later in the relationship, when you have been emailing for awhile or perhaps when you are at the telephone stage. You will also want to be watching for these words in the profiles of your prospects that you are evaluating.

These words include: passion, hugging, belly-rubbing, affection, intimacy, kissing, closeness and any reference to a "physical" relationship. There are others, but these tend to be the most common. When you think about it, there is really little reason to include any of these words in the profile you are writing. Why take the risk of sending the wrong message out to <u>all</u> potential partners? Save that conversation for someone who has become important to you and for later in the relationship. You'll be glad you did!

The Finer Points of Writing Your Essay

When I talk about your profile in this section, I am referring to the essay portion of your online resume; the part that gives most people "the willies." Most sites have you answer a number of multiple choice questions, a few short-answer questions, then write what many call an "essay", often in response to a particular question, such as "Describe yourself." (This is beginning to sound a bit like high school, isn't it? Don't you wish you had paid more attention?)

Few people are concerned about completing the multiple choice and short answer responses that are commonly included in most online sites. The part of this process that stops most people cold is the idea of writing something clever and creative about themselves that is likely to attract the sort of relationship they want. I have one client that has showed up with her profile each week for a month and the bulk of our time is spent crafting what she wants to say! We are making progress but are not there yet.

I don't mean to imply that you need to spend this much time and energy writing your essay, but you do want to give it a bit of attention before you log on. This example would be an extreme situation and I don't want you to use it as an excuse to prevent yourself from getting online. Remember, your profile is not carved in granite. If you don't like it once it's up, or it's not garnering you the type of responses you had hoped for, you can always log on and change it!

In fact, it tends to be a good idea to think of your essay as a work in progress. Keep it updated; change it occasionally. Experiment by focusing on different interests or various aspects of your personality each time. Do remember to use humor. Most prospects find that very attractive. Have fun with it. See the example in Appendix C for a simple example of a response to an essay question. I was able to write this in about ten minutes. Remember, this is **not** rocket science! Nor is it carved in stone; you can change it at any time.

Finally, now that we have covered many of the relationship-focused aspects of the profile, I want to turn our attention to the marketing component. There are several separate parts to most profiles, in addition to the statement that you make, that bear individual discussion. We will explore each of these components below.

Making a Name for Yourself

Virtually all dating sites ask you to create a user name to protect your privacy and prevent you from having to give out your real name over the web to strangers. This is simply a short name or phrase, typically posted above your photo, if you have one, that usually describes something about you. You will want to make the most of this often disregarded opportunity.

Your goal in coming up with this name should be to share something about yourself and grab the attention of the reader. You will want to set yourself apart from the others on the web and give some information about who you are since this is the first thing people will see.

Each website may have its own word for this name, but you will know it as it will be the name by which you are referred to on their site. Some of the more common names for this are your "alias," your "handle," and your "screen name."

You will want to spend some time selecting a name for yourself, as this name becomes part of the ad itself. It conveys meaning and can attract or repel potential partners. For example, notice the difference in how you may feel toward someone who calls himself, "John the Plumber" versus "One True Romantic." One has more of a definite pull to it and draws you toward him, where the other is more neutral or, perhaps to some, negative.

Take a look at what others have used in their profiles to get some ideas of qualities you can use for your own name. Be creative and try to put your own twist on what you learn. Be careful, however, because you are marketing yourself. If you say, "FunGirl" or "PartyBoy" you will probably attract a lot of partners simply looking for a good time.

The most important thing you want to do with your screen name is, just like with your ad, to create interest. Avoid very bland names, such as "Dog Lover" or "Cindy 2004." Names that are too direct, such as "MarryMe" often give the wrong message as well as scare away potential partners.

There are a number of ways to come up with an intriguing screen name. One of the easiest is to highlight your best or most alluring feature. Some examples of this type of name would include Green-eyedLady" and "MuscleMan." Get some input from a close friend if you are unable to decide on which feature you want to highlight.

Another focus for an alias can be an interest or talent you have which would, again, share a little something about you. Names such as "DrummerGirl" or "GolfGuy" fall into this category. Sports are another resource for names. "RunningLady" and "SkiBoy" are two good options. If you enjoy dancing you might use "DancingGirl" or "SalsaGuy." Take a moment to think about the things you are interested in and see if you can't come up with a name for yourself out of one of your interests.

A third focus for a name could be the type of date or relationship you are seeking. "BeachGirl" or "HarleyRider" give an indication about what type of date the owners may enjoy. Be certain if you use an interest that it is something you are truly passionate about because it will probably attract persons with like interests as well as exclude those who do not enjoy them. If it is not truly a passion for you, don't take the risk of alienating potential partners. Also, names such as "JustDivorced" or "SeriousLady" might indicate the type of relationship you are, and are not, seeking.

Another type of alias is something that only another person with a similar interest would understand, such as a reference to an obscure Star Trek episode or a Star Wars character. I can't give you an example because I don't have these interests myself, but those of you with these areas of interest can understand my meaning and probably do a bang up job creating a clever name. If you do, and you care to share it for the next edition of this book, please contact me at the email address in Appendix B. I would appreciate it.

Names such as these would also give you something to talk about when you begin to converse, both online and on the telephone. They act as an ice breaker and you will know immediately you have an interest in common. You might also use the name of an actor or author that you enjoy, such as "JohnGrishamFan" to attract persons with like interests.

The bottom line in developing the screen name or alias is to be creative and have fun. You can always try a name out and see the response it gets. Most sites have procedures for changing your name or creating a new profile when you want to make a change, so whatever name you choose is, again, not carved in stone. Just keep in mind the message you convey with the name you choose.

Writing the "Hook"

In addition to a clever user name, most sites require you to write what they call a "headline" to be placed at the top of your ad or profile. You will want to put careful thought into this as well, because it will define the type of partner you attract. On some sites, potential dates will see only this headline, or hook, and must then "click" on it to visit your profile.

Design the headline to say something about you and to grab attention. The more people it intrigues, the more potential partners view your profile. Think of this as similar to creating your alias, but a little longer with a few more words, but with the same kind of goal to draw people in to your profile. Issuing a challenge, asking a question or creating curiosity can be a good hook.

Some examples include:
♡ "Are You Adventurous?"
♡ "How About a Walk on the Beach at Sunset?"
♡ "Let's Get to Know Each Other"
♡"Sunrise or Sunset?"

♡ "Write to me in French"
♡ "Coffee or Juice?"

Similar to the name, the "hook" is designed to pull someone in, to trigger an interest the two of you share. The best ads are clever, fun, spark an interest and give someone a sense of your personality. Use the headline to do this. Think of it as an ad slogan for your profile or a catch phrase that sums up your personality and grabs the attention of the reader. Headlines can make the initial dating process easier and more interactive. Again, think carefully about the type of interest you want to trigger because the types of relationships you attract will depend on the suggestions you make in your headline.

A Clever Conclusion

The final component of the profile essay that I want to discuss individually is the conclusion. In any type of writing it is important to have a conclusion in which you ask for what you want. In sales, you call it the close.

I was helping my seventeen year old daughter draft her personal statement for college admission this week and, when first proofreading her paper, realized that she had made a very nice statement about her interests and abilities, and then it just stopped dead. There was no conclusion. So I suggested she go back and add a paragraph at the end asking for what she wanted. She brought it back with a beautiful conclusion summarizing her desire to attend that school and why she thought she would be a good candidate for them to choose, i.e. the close.

In your profile, in addition to asking for what you want, the conclusion also has another task. Similar to the alias and the hook, it should also grab attention and create interest or intrigue. Issuing an invitation or a challenge can be effective conclusion. Statements such as, "Contact me to see what you've been missing" or "Let's get to know each other better — are you willing?" can accomplish this purpose.

Again, it is a good idea to take a look online and see what types of conclusions other persons are using and add your own twist to one of those. Be careful, again, of the message you are sending. Will it lead to the type of relationship you are seeking? Take another look at the sample profile in Appendix C. Does the conclusion create interest? Issue an invitation? Is it effective? Think about how you can do this with your own essay.

Other Issues

There are a couple of other points about writing a profile that I would like to address here. These are just some general ideas on what to say and how to say it, but do not fit into the individual categories discussed above. Keep these thoughts in mind as you respond to both the multiple choice and the essay questions.

Express Yourself

Your essay should express something about who you are. The body of the profile, the part between the headline and the conclusion, should contain a few sentences about you, your interests and the type of relationship you are seeking. All of those things we listed at the beginning of this chapter. You want to give some thought to how you express yourself there as well.

Some people drag themselves to online dating as if they were marching to their execution and this comes through in their ads. They have no energy and they are unlikely to attract positive and fulfilling relationships. Ignite your creativity, put some energy into your profile, have fun with it. There is nothing more fulfilling than creating something that expresses who you are clearly and having fun while you do it.

You can always change your profile as well so don't delay or hold out for the perfect ad. Simply take your best shot now and if the perfect inspiration occurs to you in two weeks, go ahead and change it. You may want to may revisions based on the feedback you get as well. Remember, your profile is not carved in stone, but is yours to remold and recreate as you wish.

Too Much of a Good Thing

Some people, in a desperate attempt to hook or include all possible potential partners, try to list everything they enjoy doing in their profile so it becomes an overwhelming laundry list of activities. List a few of your most important interests, perhaps with a brief word or two about how you became interested in it, such as the fact that you enjoy running because you like to challenge yourself individually. You just want to convey a main idea or two, not give your life history.

If you are a woman, this point is especially important. You need to understand that male and female brains work differently. While, on some level we have always known this, they are doing some fascinating research on brain structure and function these days that bears this out.

One of the most interesting discoveries to come out of this research is that men do better at focusing intently on one or, perhaps, two areas or tasks at a time, while women can more easily juggle or hold in their awareness a number of ideas at once. A woman can more easily access multiple bits of information very quickly, though she typically does not maintain as intense a focus as the male on his task.

This typically leads to a division of function by skill. A simple example of this appears in the days of the cave man. Men typically had one function: to hunt. They most often hunted in a pack, following a lead hunter and their focus was intense.

The women, on the other hand, were charged with a number of different tasks or functions at the same time, though none typically as intense and constant as the hunt. Women were expected to gather food, mind the cave, tend the fire and care for the children. As you can see, in some ways little has changed.

To illustrate further how this affects us today and why it may be important in a dating relationship, most of my female clients can quickly access information about any of these functions at a given moment. They can typically tell me which child has what activity on which night, how each is doing in school, what is in the refrigerator and cupboard as we speak, what tasks remain undone at home and what projects are on their desks at work. A man can typically focus on only one of these areas at a time and will need some time to shift his attention from one to the other and perhaps consult his calendar or a note from his wife. But, again, as he is attempting to access this information, his focus is typically intense.

What does this have to do with online dating? Well, to make a long story short, if you write a laundry list of activities attempting to show a potential date all of your interests, his eyes may glaze over and he may miss the one area that can best connect you to each other. You will get better results if you list two or three areas of interest that give an idea of your personality and leave the rest for subsequent communications.

Show Your Stuff

Use the body of the ad, the essay, to give a true sense of your personality. Don't just say you are a clever guy or a funny lady; give an example in your ad with a clever play on words or a witty story, especially one involving yourself (humility is a very attractive quality in a partner). This also can show that you don't take yourself too seriously and convey self confidence.

Use Humor

The world these days is a very serious place and "funny" can be very attractive. I would not try to be humorous with the "big" questions, such as filling your essay with witty quips; that can simply be irritating. But I would strongly encourage you to interject a note of humor into your responses and into your essay. Both men and women tend to like someone who can make them laugh or smile. Show your sense of humor and make it work for you.

Speak with Confidence

As we noted in the beginning, most people share similar feelings and fears about getting into the world of online dating. You are not alone. For a wide variety of reasons, online dating has become the wave of the future as far as meeting new partners is concerned. Know this and use this information to talk yourself through your initial uncertainty about taking this step. Then, speak with confidence in your profile and your communications online. Remember, you are in charge of who you talk to and how much you share with them. In many ways, computer dating is so much safer than past alternatives, such as singles' bars and blind dates.

Regarding Money

Many sites and profiles ask for information about money and employment. These are essentially two separate issues. While potential partners will want to know if you have a job and can support yourself and your needs, you really do not need to share the specific amount of money you earn. Further, many people are uncomfortable sharing this specific information very early in the relationship. For this reason, many sites will break income down into ranges so you do not need to give an actual number when completing a profile.

While many people will give their income and many others are comfortable indicating an income range, I have seen some individuals state that they prefer not to because they do not believe that a person with a higher income should be valued more in terms of partnership potential than one with a lesser income. An individual stating this preference should likewise decline receiving or requesting specific income information from potential partners for the same reason.

It is also helpful and reassuring, when stating a position such as the above, objecting to the valuing of relationship potential on income figures, to indicate that your income is sufficient to meet your needs. This way readers of your profile will know you are not looking for a partner to support you. These two statements, in combination, can be a positive and effective way to handle the issue of money.

Regarding Personal Statistics

Many sites ask very personal questions about height and weight. Some persons are uncomfortable providing this information to virtual strangers, not to mention the World Wide Web. Often, persons will vary their numbers, increasing height and decreasing weight and age. Men are most likely to increase height while women are most likely to decrease weight.

I have had clients tell me, especially men, that they have been very surprised upon meeting the women they have been corresponding with, due to weight figures being, at times, grossly under-inflated. This does not tend to have a positive effect on the future of the relationship. It, in fact, sets a tone of mistrust and distrust between the parties. When it happens so early in the relationship, this can be difficult to overcome.

It is understandable to have a certain healthy reluctance to share very personal information such as height and weight with strangers. Similar to the money issue, however, there are some positive ways to handle this without violating trust or your own values and beliefs.

One appropriate response is included in the Sample Profile in Appendix D. It reads, "While I have no objection to providing this information at a later date, and have included a recent photograph of myself, I believe that a person is more than the sum of his parts so would prefer not to give specific numbers at this point. Suffice it to say I am over the age of consent."

With a bit of humor, and the reassurance of a recent photograph, the uncomfortable moment is alleviated with grace and honesty. And by a recent photo, I would mean one taken within the past year.

Another positive response would be to provide these answers in an age or weight range or use a descriptive comment such as Rubenesque in response to the appearance questions. These comments give the reader a general idea, without an exact number, which can feel like a personal violation at this stage of contact. Again, a general idea of body style or appearance is really all the information you want or need. Most partners don't really care about a potential partner's exact height, weight or age anyway. If a man is interested in a partner with a waiflike appearance, you don't have to identify your exact weight for both of you to figure out you are not the right woman for him. A description will easily accomplish this intended purpose.

Age

Age is another piece of very personal information typically included in many profiles. Most people have less reluctance to share this, because age is of less significance these days than it may have been in the past.

If you are uncomfortable sharing your exact age, you can quote a range here as well, or if you appear much younger than your years, feel free to indicate that. Be aware that this is a common statement made by online daters, however, and many of my clients have expressed disagreement with statements made online such as "50 but look 40" so be sure to get some neutral feedback before posting this to avoid embarrassment. After all, age is only a number. You're as young as you feel!

Sample Profiles

As I stated previously, I have included a sample profile in Appendix C in the format described in this chapter. Read it over, again looking at the suggestions for how to create such a statement about yourself.

In the two Appendices (D and E) that follow, I have also included sample profiles in a different format so that several problematic issues could be addressed. You may want to read over all three samples prior to attempting your own, but don't let them prevent you from taking a stab at writing something about yourself. To get into the game, you first must be listed online.

Remember, your profile is not carved in stone once it is posted. If you follow a site over time, you will notice that most people revise or at least "tweak" their profiles periodically, so if you post something and you don't like how it comes across, or you find you are not getting the responses you had hoped for, change it.

Most Common Mistakes Made

Listed below are five of the most common mistakes or ways that people get themselves into trouble in terms of how they create their profiles. I list them here to make you aware of them as you create your own, but many of these have been discussed at length previously in this chapter in the sections on how to do things right, so if you identify any of these errors, you will also want to re-read sections of the chapter pertaining to that issue.

♡ Too Much Information

Listing every possible activity of interest is a mistake many online daters make. This overwhelms potential partners and can obscure the information that can attract the right partner. List one or two activities; keep your profile short and to the point. Hit the highlights; don't tell your life story.

♡ CAPITALIZING EVERYTHING!

Some people, in an attempt to emphasize their profile or make a point in a later email contact, make the mistake of capitalizing much or all of what they type. This is usually a turn-off because it tends to make people feel they are being SCREAMED AT ALL THE TIME! Don't use this tactic to get attention; it will likely get you a negative response.

♡ Talking About Past Relationships

This is a red flag to many people because it can indicate that you are not ready for any kind of relationship. After all, if you have two minutes of someone's time, why waste it talking about someone else? Focus on yourself and your interests. You can always get into the past further into the relationship if there is a reason to.

♡ Being Very Negative

People who are very negative and cynical are no fun to be around. A lot of negativity in a profile is a turn-off to potential readers. Try to see the glass as half-full when you are writing your ad. Focus on the positive and you are more likely to have positive results.

One other point about negativity in general: persons who are very negative often find themselves the victim of one negative experience after another. Seeing themselves as the victim of life's experiences, they often bring on other negative experiences for themselves.

For one thing, you tend to get and see more of what you pay attention to. If you believe the glass is half empty, all of life can feel that way to you. If, instead, you focus on the glass being half full, you will see more of the positives in life and find yourself more grateful for the gifts you do receive. You will then, in turn, attract more positive experiences and people to you, leading to more to be grateful for.

We have a choice. Why not choose to be happy?

"You are a living magnet.
What you attract into your life
is in harmony with your dominant thoughts."

~Brian Tracy

♡ Moving Too Fast (MarryMe)

Moving too fast feels desperate and frightens people away. A handle such as "MarryMe" should be a huge red flag and typically indicates someone who feels too inadequate about himself to truly be a partner to anyone. Proposing after a few "chats" or saying "I love you" after a few dates are red flags that come up a bit later in the relationship. Don't make these mistakes. Take it slowly and, if you are tempted to do either of these things, jump quickly to Chapter Seven.

Get Some Feedback

Once you have your profile put together, especially your alias, headline and conclusion, show it to several people before you post it online to get some objective feedback about how you are coming across. If you are sending messages you are not intending to send, perhaps your readers can give you some constructive tips on how to change your message as well.

Who to contact? There are three main resources for feedback: friends, co-workers and your therapist, if you are working with one. Friends can be a wonderful resource, provided they can be objective and neutral enough to not just tell you what you want to hear or say positive things because they love you. Think carefully about who you will show your profile to and assess how much value you can give what they will tell you.

Co-workers can be a good resource for this type of feedback because they are often more neutral then friends. You will often get a more accurate picture of the image you are sending from a co-worker, provided your work environment is supportive to online dating, either formally or informally. Co-workers can also be wonderful resources for constructive criticism when something needs to be changed as well.

If you are working with a therapist, I cannot recommend strongly enough that you share your profile with her and ask for suggestions. She is probably aware of relationship issues you have dealt with in the past and can guide you into successfully avoiding them this time around.

Jenny, the woman you will meet in the example at the beginning of Chapter Four, chose not to include her picture in her initial profile because we had been working in therapy on her relying on her looks to find partners, which had lead to a series of destructive relationships. She ultimately came to the conclusion that she wanted to post her profile without a photo. This was an important part of her therapy and an important component of the relationship she eventually found.

Debbie, another of my clients, brought her profile to a session and we discussed it at length. Debbie had been in a series of relationships with abusive partners and there were some red flags in her profile and those of the men she was attracted to that we were able to discuss so that she would be more likely to avoid a future abusive relationship.

I am not suggesting that you must be in therapy in order to participate safely in online dating. But if you are in therapy already, or are thinking about getting into therapy for any reason, invite your therapist to assist you in completing your profile. You'll be glad you did!

There is a lot of material covered in this chapter and it may feel overwhelming your first time through. It would be a good idea to read over the chapter again before actually completing your profile to review the most important concepts. Also, take a look at the summary on the following page and use it to help identify any sections of the chapter you may want to re-read.

Good Luck creating a winning profile!

"Too many people overvalue what they are not and undervalue what they are."

~Malcolm Forbes

"Once Upon a Time" Summary

♡**Marketing Yourself**

What positive qualities do you possess?

_____

_____

_____

What qualities might someone look for in a partner?

_____

_____

_____

What do you want in a relationship?

_____

_____

_____

♡**The Approach:**

~Be Clear   ~Be Positive

~Be Honest   ~Be Respectful

♡**The Finer Points of Writing Your Essay**

My alias will be:

_____

My headline will be:

_____

I will conclude with:

_____

♡**Other Issues:**

~Express yourself   ~Speak with confidence

~Keep it brief   ~The money issue

~Show your stuff   ~Personal statistics

~Use humor   ~Age is only a number

♡**Most Common Profile Mistakes**

~Too much information   ~Being negative

~CAPITALIZING!   ~Moving too fast

~Talking about past relationships

♡**Get Some Neutral Feedback!**

Chapter 4

To See or Not To See

The Decision to Include a Photo

46 ❙ *'m just not sure about the picture thing,"* comments *Jenny during one of our sessions.*

"What do you mean, Jenny?" I respond, wanting her to articulate this, because it was something we had been working on in her therapy, but understanding where she was going with it.

"Well, I've always relied on my looks to get a relationship. I've been the cute cheerleader, the blonde bombshell, the party girl. But every guy I've dated has been attracted by my looks and I want a deeper relationship than that. I want somebody who likes and is attracted to the "me" inside, not just my Barbie doll looks. I'm afraid to use a picture because I won't know whether it's the outside me or the inside me that they're wanting to get to know."

The majority of persons engaging in online dating do choose to include at least one photo of themselves as part of their profile. You will want to give some thought to the issue of whether or not you want to do so, as well as the reasoning for your choice. In addition, should you decide to add a photo to your ad, you will want to choose carefully the one you include. We will explore these issues in this chapter to help you make informed choices.

Including a Photo

As stated above, the majority of profiles you will find online will include a photo. Some people assume you are required to include one; others just do it because it seems to be expected. There are some good reasons to post a photo if you are comfortable doing so.

First of all, anyone observing a profile with no photo will be inclined to wonder why it was not included. They may also be likely to conclude that the candidate is horribly unattractive or, faced with the choice of a less attractive profile that did include a photo, be unwilling to take the chance on the prospect with no picture. In short, eliminating the photo from your profile can work to your detriment if no reason for doing so is included as an explanation, whether it is financial ("Am saving to buy a digital camera") or philosophical (see Jenny's example at the beginning of this chapter).

It is commonly thought among the online daters that I work with that if you don't include a photo, you will get few "hits," i.e. people hitting your profile. According to one male client, Dave, "You won't get **any**one if you don't have a picture." While I am not certain this is accurate, I believe that omitting the photo would at least beg the question of why it is absent. I am aware of this because this is exactly the sentiment by my clients on the receiving end of photo-less profiles.

Another reason to include the photo is that, even if you are not a great beauty or handsome hunk, (and, let's face it, how many of us fit those criteria?) it is reassuring to readers to get a look at you. People like to have a feel and a sense of what someone looks like before contacting them. I have heard and seen this response from my clients as well. In looking at some photos of potential dates who were very average looking, I hear comments such as, "He looks nice," or "She seems like she could be a nice person." It can relieve a lot of anxiety about the online dating process to have a photo to look at.

Going Photo-Less

My best argument for going photo-less is the profound example of Jenny at the beginning of this chapter. It was a pivotal moment in her therapy when, at the end of the session described above, she could say to me, "I don't want to include my photo in my profile because I don't want to get another relationship based on my appearance."

Jenny followed that experience by getting involved in three reasonably successful relationships, all of which were healthy and fulfilling for her. She is still involved with the last of these three partners and each of them "hit" on her profile even though it included no photo. I think she may have included a brief comment in her profile about the reason for her choice. What a wonderful ice-breaker! If you make the same decision Jenny did, you can be sure anyone who contacts you is responding to the marketing information created by the inner-you and not just your outer appearance.

Another reason to decline to include a photo is a lack of equipment and resources. Perhaps you do not own a digital camera and are saving up from your divorce to purchase one. Perhaps you have recently relocated and do not have any friends or acquaintances who could take the picture for you. A brief note about these circumstances in your profile would be reassuring to potential partners. Further many online services will accept a regular photo that you mail to them and will scan it into your profile.

Some people are reluctant to use a photo because they are embarrassed about being involved in online dating. However, the only folks who will be seeing your picture have made the same choice. If that is your excuse, what do you have to lose? If you are afraid of being recognized in your home town, read on!

Other Options

There are several other options for making a photo available online but which alleviate or minimize the difficulties associated with some of the reasoning for not posting a photo with your profile.

Posting on Another Web Page

One option for getting around the photo issue involves using a Web site that posts your photo but is only accessible to those to whom you provide the web address. You can provide this information when you email a potential date by adding a statement to your message similar to: "I didn't post my photo because…(state your reason here)…, but you can see it at www.xyz.com/photohost. If you go to that site, you will be able to see some pictures of me."

Always include this note and address with your first message. Potential dates will probably be hesitant to ask for photos for fear of appearing shallow. If you do not send the address right away, they may just drift away. Offering to send them a photo or the address is not the same thing and will typically not have the same effect. Remember you are competing with millions of other prospects, many of whom already have a photo available online. Thus, you get more mileage out of this option if you include it with your very first contact.

When choosing a web site to host your photo, make sure you understand the terms. Some sites offer this service free of charge, others do require a fee. Further, when posting on some sites, you are granting the right for them to sell your photo. You will also want to explore and understand the procedure for deleting your photo and closing your account and making sure that this is something you will be able to do. Check each of these issues out carefully prior to posting on the web.

You can also set up your own web site to host your photo. This will remain secure. The drawbacks are that it will involve more effort and a greater cost on your part.

The other drawback to this option is that it should be used only if you are expecting to be proactive and email anyone you would like to date. We know from experience that many online daters will not contact someone who has no photo posted so you will likely lose some daters that may otherwise reach out to you.

Posting Outside your Hometown

Another option, if you are afraid of being recognized in your hometown if you post your photo online, is to post your profile from a different community or zip code when registering. The main drawback would be that you may not get emails from singles in your community who may dismiss you as a prospect because of your distance from them.

Again, if you are using this option, you will want to be proactive in contacting persons from your community as they probably will not be contacting you. Include a message in your first email saying something like, "I know it looks like I'm from Madison, but I really live in Green Bay. I posted myself in Madison because too many people know me in my community. I can explain more when you write to me."

This technique can come across as slightly sneaky or untrustworthy. That is why it is important to come clean right away and explain why you are making this choice and in which community you truly live. If you wait several weeks before sharing that you are really living in the same community as your potential partner, trust will and should become as issue in any potential relationship you develop.

Making Your Own Decision

Whether you choose to include a photo or not, is completely up to you. There are valid and acceptable reasons to make either choice. The important thing is to be comfortable with your decision. In doing this work and preparing this profile, the person you want to please is yourself. There are no right or wrong answers.

Above all you will want to pay attention to your gut reaction to any of the choices you make throughout your online dating experience and, indeed, throughout your life. Your gut reaction is something that most of us are very aware of as children, but it is gradually socialized or trained out of us by people we come in contact with. Consider a child going to school for the first time. Upon being prepared to walk out the door, his immediate reaction might be, "Mommy I'm afraid to go to school." "No, you're not afraid, honey, you'll be fine," is typically the response he receives. He is being told to deny what he is feeling inside. And, indeed, who among us was not scared going to school for the first time? We are leaving all that is comfortable and familiar and going into a strange environment with people we have never met. This is just one of many experiences that we encounter in the name of socialization or behavior management that teach us to deny our instincts.

This gut instinct that I am talking about can guide you in many situations if you can get in touch with it. This is the feeling that something is not right when you are walking down a dark street at night. It is this that makes you pick up the phone just at the time someone needs to hear your voice.

Several months ago, my daughter was driving home after dark from a friend's home in a neighboring town. I had the feeling I should give her a call, so I picked up the phone. She said, "Hi Mom, I'm about a half hour away. Oh my god, I'm going to hit a deer!" She was able to slow the car down and hit him at a slow speed, but was hyperventilating in the car afterwards. I was able to talk her through some deep breathing exercises and calm her down and she was able to drive herself home. If I had not called her, I doubt she would have been able to reach out to me at that moment. Often it is with loved ones, that we especially notice this gut reaction coming into play. But, whenever you are making a decision, your gut instinct will likely be able to give you some feedback, if you let it. Train yourself to pay attention to it and let it guide you. You won't be disappointed.

In making your decision about the photo, think about how you feel. List the pros and cons (for you) of including a photo in your profile. Make your best choice. You can always change your mind and add or delete the picture later, depending on the responses you are getting.

The Photo You Choose to Include

When you do choose to include a photo, think again about marketing. After all, you are marketing **yourself** and you are **in** the market for a partner or a relationship. Think carefully about the image you wish to portray.

Get Some Feedback

Get some feedback from the people you spoke with in Chapter Three about the photo or photos you are thinking of including on your site. If your friend or co-worker will simply give you a one word answer such as, "Nice," or "Fine," in response to a photo, try asking a question about the photo. Ask them, "If you had to describe this photo (or the person in it) with one or two words, what would it be?"

If you are male, it is good to get a female perspective on your photo and if you are female, ask a male for input. Remember who you are trying to attract. It is helpful to know how you are coming across to the opposite sex.

What you are looking for is how the photo portrays you and this is often difficult to determine about yourself. You want to know if you come across as "serious," "elegant," "fun to be with," "nice," "sophisticated," "stuck up," or "easy." Perhaps reading her this list can give your friend the idea of what you are looking for. Above all, you want her to be honest and to give you more perspective than you will likely have viewing your own photo.

When you get the feedback you're asking for, think about whether the image that is coming across is the one you want to portray. This is a very personal decision. However, a person who appears sophisticated will typically attract different types of potential dates than someone who seems "nice" or "fun to be with." If your photo is sending a different message than you want to be sending, change it and get more feedback.

Make Sure to Use a Current Photo

We all have pictures of ourselves from 20 years ago that we may like better than those of today. DO NOT use them. Use a current photo for best results. Current photos are less than a year old.

You may like how you look better in the old photograph, but eventually, if the relationship takes off as you hope it will, you will meet in person. You may look terrific today, but you no longer look like you did 20 years ago. Expectations can be dashed and trust destroyed if photographs do not truly represent the person who shows up.

A client of mine, Kelly, is an incredibly beautiful 55 year old woman. Truth to tell, she looks more like 45 than 55 and could honestly be described as stunning. On her profile she had posted a photo of herself taken approximately 15-20 years ago, which does not, in reality, resemble her. I actually think she is more beautiful today than in her photograph. Her online dating experience is to get a lot of "hits" with whom she eventually meets up, only to have them disappear after two or three dates. Her photo is a problem and I have advised her of this, but to date she has retained the picture.

Another client, Doug, has made the comment to me that he has discovered that in most cases, the women he eventually meets do not resemble their online photos much at all. This has been a disappointment for him and has caused him to have some difficulty developing trust in these relationships.

It Should be a Good Representation of You

Make sure the photo you use looks like you and is large and close enough to show that likeness. Include a standard head and shoulders shot, as there is usually little space available. Avoid a full body shot and do not show just your face. Because of the lack of space and distractibility, do not include other persons or pets in the photo. For the same reason, make sure the background is not overly busy or distracting. You want to give your potential dates a sense of who you are so focus on showing just that.

Your dress should be business casual or just casual rather than formal or business attire. Blue jeans are fine as long as they are neat and clean and dressed up with a nice shirt or blouse, especially if you wear jeans regularly. Be sure to wear a color that is complementary to you. Get some input from a friend if you are unsure what colors look best on you. You may need to take a number of photographs to get two or three you are comfortable with.

It Should be a Tasteful Photo

In choosing the photo you will use, make sure it is tasteful. In making your selection, ask yourself if you would be comfortable with a potential partner taking the photo home to mother or showing it to co-workers. Most of the clients I work with and with whom I discuss online dating have at one time or another brought in a profile photo off the internet. You just never know where those pictures may turn up so choose wisely.

Pay attention to the message your clothes are sending. Women should be careful of low necklines and short skirt lengths; men want to be sure to wear clothing clean and in good shape, free of rips and tears.

Pose is important too. Avoid anything too suggestive or aggressive. You don't want to be selling anything too overtly online.

How Many Should You Post?

Many sites give you the opportunity to post more than one photo. Take the opportunity to do so if offered, using different angles, outfits, locations or activities. If you post, it is usually a good idea to include two different shots to give more of a complete representation of yourself.

This is an especially good idea if one of the photos is a bit older, so you can provide a reassuringly current photo of yourself. While an obvious choice would be not to use an older

photo, some persons have a favorite photo of themselves that is
a bit out of date. Posting two pictures is a good way to use the
preferred photo, but to give current information as well.
A common mistake when posting multiple photos is to
include several photos in the same outfit, pose and location.
Men are more like to commit this *faux pas*. There is really
nothing to gain by this as you are showing the same view of
yourself multiple times.

When you choose or shoot the photos, make sure to
change outfits, one in casual clothing or involved in a sport
and one in business or more professional attire, perhaps
something you would wear to work, are good choices. You are
trying to give a viewer a composite view of you as well as a
taste of your personality. Thinking about it in these terms may
help to focus your search for just the right photograph to
include.

Some sites let you post as many photos as you care to.
Be a bit cautious here. Anything over two, or at the most three,
can appear arrogant. Posting six or eight photos online can say
to a prospect, "Look at me; see how attractive I am." Even if
that is what you want them to think, be cautious about shoving
it in their faces. That's a real turn-off and is likely to lose you
more dates than it attracts.

A Few Final Thoughts About Photos

Some people recommend having professional photos taken to
put in your profile. This is entirely up to you. Many people use
digital photos taken by a friend in their own home and have
fine results. Scanned photos are fine as long as they are of good
quality. The choice is yours. You do want to avoid looking
overly "done up", however, as is the case in most glamour-
type photos.

Some online daters are cautious about a photo that
appears professionally taken or like a glamour shot, even if it is
not overdone. The reason for this is that these photos may bear
little resemblance to what the person actually looks like. If you

do include a professional or glamour shot, it can be a good idea to include a more natural, casual photo of yourself as well.

Some advisors recommend having hair professionally styled for the photo. This is a personal choice as well. I have seen some photos with hair casually styled at home that I liked better and found more flattering than photos with professionally styled hair. If you are more comfortable going to your stylist, by all means do so. But do not feel obligated to do so if you feel you can do an adequate job at home. After all, having your hair the way you normally wear it is more likely to give a better representation of the "real you" than a styled shot.

The final comment is about facial expression. Your expression should be pleasant and should involve a nice, not forced, smile. Show some teeth if you can possibly do so and maintain a genuine smile. Make sure your smile carries throughout your face and into your eyes. If your mouth is smiling, but your face is tense and your eyes look dead, you won't carry the look off. You will look angry or irritated, rather than pleasant and relaxed. Have a friend tell you jokes until you can achieve and maintain a real smile long enough to be captured on film.

In general, most online daters do find that it is helpful to include a photo. It can reassure potential partners that you are a "normal human being" and have nothing to hide. Even if you are not a handsome hunk or raving beauty, it can draw prospects to you so I would strongly encourage posting at least one photo in most cases.

If your reluctance is similar to my client Jenny's, I would certainly address or explain this briefly in my profile. This is easy to understand and can operate to reassure those reluctant to contact anyone without a photo.

In addition, posting a photo with your profile can provide a sense of comfort and familiarity that can carry over into your communication with each other. Do, however, spend some time carefully choosing the photo to be included. Finally, if you find you are attracting the wrong sort of person, take a look at your photo to see if it could be sending the wrong message.

In choosing or evaluating a photo, remember, most people look better than their worst picture and worse than their best. If you can keep this in mind while evaluating your own photos, as well as those of your prospects, you will have an easier time choosing what to post and are not likely to be shocked when you meet your date in person!

Take a look, also, at the summary on the following page to review some of the most important aspects of the decision to include a photo. And **SMILE!**

"The man who trims himself to suit everybody will soon whittle himself away."

~Charles Schwab

"To See or Not to See" Summary

♡   In most cases, including a photo with your profile will get you more prospects.

♡   There are some good reasons to go "photo-less", however. If you make this choice, address it in your profile.

♡   Other options include:

~Posting to another web page,
~Posting outside your hometown or
~Offering to email a photo to contacts.

♡   Make your own decision regarding this important issue, paying attention to your gut instincts.

♡   Think carefully about any photo you choose to include:

~Get some feedback
~Make sure it is current
~Make certain it is a good representation of you
~Be sure it is tasteful—would you take it home to mother?
~Post one or two photos, not a dozen

♡   SMILE!

"To love oneself
is the beginning of a lifelong romance."

~Oscar Wilde

Chapter 5

What You Don't Know <u>Can</u> Hurt You

Evaluating a Profile

"Ok, what do you have for me today?"* I ask Debbie, a long time client with whom I have processed the issues of depression, work stress, a past divorce, children's adjustment to the divorce, post-divorce court proceedings, the difficulties of being an attractive single woman in a small, largely married community and, now, the mysteries of online dating.*

"Well, I brought three. But I really like the looks of this guy," she responds, handing me the photo and profile of "Rafe."*

"Hmmm," is all the response I immediately muster while taking in the photo of the attractive man who appears in a dirty and torn t-shirt, standing next to his motorcycle with uncombed hair and a cigarette hanging out of his mouth. "Let's take a look at his profile."*

"It looks pretty good," she prompts hopefully, "He has a full time job and makes a pretty good income."*

"Let's see: 'Describe your childhood: violent and dysfunctional; Relationship with family of origin: none; Hobbies and interests:

drinking and partying...Debbie we need to talk; I have some concerns here."

Where do I begin?

I really had a session very similar to that described in this example. While the profile seems obviously disturbing, Debbie who is a very attractive, intelligent woman with a college degree and a good job was not immediately aware of the dangers. I have seen this time and again. In the hopes of finding Mr. or Ms. Right (yes, I have seen this blindness from my male clients as well), reasonable and intelligent people overlook some of the most basic red flags and warning signs.

The purpose of this chapter and Appendices D and E in the back of this book is to teach you to become more aware of what to steer clear of in a potential partner's profile, as well as what to investigate further.

Common Warning Signs

I would like to begin by discussing some of the more common red flags or warning signs found in online dating profiles. Each speaks volumes about the writer, if you know what to look for. With the goal of helping you to become an astute judge of profile character and more aware of some problem areas, let's begin.

Negative Comments and Judgments About Others

While it may seem obvious that negative comments about others are a warning sign, this may be done with great subtlety and finesse. Certainly, any name calling or blaming is cause for concern, such as referring to family members or former partners as "losers" or chalking up a childhood as dysfunctional.

Ideally we would see a writer acknowledging problems earlier in life, but taking responsibility for figuring things out, working through problems and taking steps to avoid repeating the same mistakes in the future. If the profile contains sarcasm, especially in reference to a loved one or family or relationship experience, this can portend how you will be represented (or **mis**represented) to future partners. Remember, what you are seeing is likely to be a relationship pattern. It **is** likely to repeat itself.

Further, referring to others in general in detrimental terms indicates a lack of empathy and respect that is also likely to be visited upon you if you involve yourself with this person. Persons who are able to feel and show empathy for others are likely to be able to carry that over to all relationships and contacts about them, such as an online profile. These qualities should be apparent upon reading a profile, if they are there.

Past Partners or Relationships

Watch how former spouses or partners are referred to if they are mentioned. Remember, this could be you one day. How she talks about persons she used to be involved with is likely to continue and can give you much information about your future with this person.

In addition, look for indications that he takes some responsibility and shows some insight into his role in the ending or problems in a past relationship. If he summarizes his marriage by saying, "The bitch ran out on me," or "It was all her fault," he is telling you he has not yet developed the ability to accept responsibility for his own contribution to these events. As such, he is likely to repeat the same mistakes. Therefore, what eventually made his former wife or partner unhappy enough to end the relationship is likely to be in your future as well. See Appendices C and D for further discussion and examples of these factors.

Arrogance

A client once brought in a profile that read something like the following:

> *"I was honored as businessman of the year by my colleagues and I built a new $300,000 home for myself last year. I am involved in community*

*theatre and was recently awarded the lead in our
next production because of my excellent singing
ability. I also won an award for my singing last
year by the XYZ group because they were so
impressed by me. I would love to meet you and
take you for a ride in my BMW; then we could
spend some time in my hot tub and I could sing
to you."*

It continued on, but after I had read that much I asked
my client if she was sure she wanted to meet this guy. She
responded, "Yes, he sounds really interesting! I'm going to
meet him this weekend."

I tried to gently suggest that he sounded pretty full of
himself, but she had her plans made and was dead set on
keeping the date. The following month, she came in to report
on her progress and made the comment, "I met that guy, but
all he could talk about was himself. Then, when we got into the
hot tub, he kept pressuring me to take my top off. When I
wouldn't, he took me home."

As I said, this is not rocket science. In most cases, the
handwriting is on the wall if you only know what to look for
and can read between the lines.

Troublesome References to Childhood and Family

Pay close attention to how a potential date refers to his
childhood and family. Negative references could represent
underlying issues that need some attention. To some extent, we
act in all of our intimate relationships in ways that were
modeled for us and engendered early in our lives. If there was
much negativity in our early life, we may have more work to
do to be able to participate in a relationship in a healthy and
respectful manner than if we had a reasonably happy and
positive childhood.

For these reasons, give particular attention to what is
said about a potential partner's early life. Family members
described as "losers" and a childhood described as
"dysfunctional" can be warning signs that new relationships
will be troubled as well. If you hear any of these negative

comments, at least inquire further to determine if there are problematic issues. At the very least, the inquiry will give you information about the sender's values and beliefs about family, loyalty and responsibility.

Focus on Alcohol and Drug Use

While many sites ask multiple choice questions about smoking and alcohol and drug use, in response to which most people will admit to "social drinking" this actually provides very little insight into an individual's personal habits. Most people assume what is acceptable to them is what is considered social drinking so the term has become virtually meaningless.

You will eventually want to inquire about habits to find out exactly what your "date" means by "social drinking." This can be a subject to investigate during your email and telephone conversations prior to actually meeting each other in person, so that you can choose wisely whether or not to take that step.

Other incidental references in the profile to alcohol, smoking and drug use can give you a more accurate picture of the person's true habits, however. If, for example, in his essay, he describes his favorite college memory as the time he and his buddies went out and got blitzed, you have a pretty clear picture of his values. If her examples of family gatherings or holiday celebrations and social events are replete with references to alcohol, the handwriting is on the wall.

Often it takes some time to ferret out if these habits will be problematic in a relationship. However, sometimes they will reveal themselves in a profile, as in the example at the beginning of this chapter. Knowing what to look for and how to interpret the information can leave you better prepared and less likely to be disappointed.

Interests and Hobbies Should Be Similar

Most sites include a question about hobbies and interests of potential partners. Pay close attention to the activities listed here and your reaction to them. If it reads like a laundry list of adventures that you would rather have a root canal than experience, do not pursue the relationship even if he is attractive and drives a BMW. You will save yourself and the other person a lot of frustration and misery in the long run.

On the other hand, if your interests and hobbies are similar, or, at the very least, some of the activities she has listed you occasionally enjoy or have always wanted to try, this can be a wonderful basis to begin a relationship. It may only take an eager interest in new adventures to convert you into a devotee of your new partner's favorite hobby.

Read the list over carefully, because much of your relationship will develop in your free time. How you are spending that time can be very important. If you are wanting to be reading quietly together in front of a crackling fire and she wants to be out snowshoeing in the blizzard, you could be in for much unhappiness. Both of you will pay a price.

Children

Children are another very important area of the profile. Most sites ask either if daters have or want children, or both. Some will even go so far as to ask if the children are living with you. This can be important to some partners. Perhaps he has no interest in children, but if the kids are adults and on their own, it becomes a less important issue.

You do want to be careful, however, if you have very disparate views regarding children and you want to clarify this at the beginning of the relationship. You don't want to keep your children a secret until the relationship is secure, because it won't be. Likewise, you don't want to keep your desire for children a secret until you have an emotional attachment. Before getting too involved, if children are an important issue for you, a deal-breaker as it were, put that out on the table.

If you have children, you will also want to get information about how your potential partner feels about them. If your site does not include questions about children and their ages and living arrangements, include this in your profile so you can save yourself the trouble of becoming involved with any partners who would be jealous and frustrated by your having and wanting to give attention to children. I know this happens because it occurs regularly with my clients. Non-child-friendly partners have gotten jealous and testy about something as simple and understandable as a mother wanting to include her 16 year old son in dinner arrangements in the home. She was faced with the question, "Why does he have to eat supper with us," forcing her to answer, "Because he's my son!" Don't go there. Get this out on the table early so you know what you're dealing with and can meet it, or avoid it, head-on.

Evasiveness

In most cases, evasiveness is a bad or negative thing in a dating profile. We will look in this section at why that is and at some forms evasiveness can take. However, it is not always a bad thing. We will also become aware of when and why it is okay to be evasive when dating online.

Work, Living Arrangements, Children, Marital Status

Here is where evasiveness or vague answers are cause for concern. When you are reading responses to questions about whether or not someone is married, has or wants children, where they live and with whom and whether they are employed, it is important to have a specific and clear response.

This is because there are several equally important aspects in a truly intimate relationship:

♡ **passion**, or the romantic, sexual part of the relationship

♡ **intimacy**, or the sharing of thoughts, feelings, hopes and dreams and

♡ **commitment** to making the relationship continue to evolve or last.

Each of these components must be met to about the same degree in order for a relationship to be healthy and fulfilling for both partners.

Underlying each component is trust. For instance, if you have passion and intimacy, but no commitment, you cannot trust your partner to be there or for your relationship to be safe, physically or emotionally. If you have intimacy and commitment, you short-circuit an important part of your life by foregoing the passionate component of your physical needs. I know there are couples out there who make do with this type of arrangement, but, as a relationship therapist, I can tell you that both partners lose something important. And, finally, if you have passion and commitment, but no intimacy as you never talk or share thoughts and feelings with each other, how fulfilling would the relationship be to you? You would have your passion and commitment needs met, but, again, your relationship is lacking a component most partners find important and necessary for true fulfillment.

In order to develop a healthy relationship and enhance the development of these crucial components, you must have information regarding the issues outlined above. After all, you cannot trust a partner, nor do you have a commitment or intimacy if you have no knowledge of whether or not she is married or single, whether she lives alone or with another man.

In addition, you have no way of knowing whether he can be a responsible partner if you have no idea if he has a job and can help contribute to the upkeep of the family. Further, action is a component of commitment. We can say we support something, but unless we take actions to do so, our commitment is just words.

Finally, knowing whether someone wants or has children is an important part of the intimacy relationship component. How can you know another's hopes and dreams, thoughts and feelings if you have no idea if they want to have children?

Each of these elements is an important one on which to receive a clear and specific answer, either in a profile or essay, or at the very least, in response to a direct question once you begin to chat. There is no room for evasiveness in these areas and any that does occur should be considered a red flag and investigated more fully before the relationship is pursued further.

Regarding Money

The issue of money is a bit different than that of employment. While you do need to know if a partner has a job and can support himself and his needs, you really do not have a need to know the specific amount of money he makes. For this reason, many sites will break income down into ranges, so you do not need to give an actual number when completing a profile.

While many people will give their income and many others are comfortable indicating an income range, I have seen some individuals state that they prefer not to because they do not believe that a person with a higher income should be valued more in terms of partnership potential than one with a lesser income. As stated previously, any individual stating this belief should likewise decline specific income information from partners for the same reason.

It is also helpful and reassuring, when stating a position such as the above objecting to the valuing of relationship potential on income figures, to indicate that your income is sufficient to meet your needs. This way readers of your profile will know you are not looking for a partner to support you. These two statements, in combination, can be a positive and effective way to handle the issue of money.

Evaluating Personal Statistics

As discussed in the previous chapter, many sites ask very personal questions about height and weight. While some of this material was covered in Chapter Three, which focused on completing your own profile, we will now explore the arena of personal statistics from the standpoint of evaluating information a potential partner has provided in his profile.

Understand first, that just as you may have been reluctant to include personal statistics when completing your own profile, many others are also uncomfortable providing this information to virtual strangers, not to mention the World Wide Web. Often, persons will vary their numbers, increasing height and decreasing weight. Again, men are most likely to increase height while women are most likely to decrease weight.

I have had clients tell me, especially men, that they have been very surprised upon meeting the women they have been corresponding with, due to weight figures being, at time, grossly under-inflated. As we discussed previously, this does not tend to have a positive effect on the future of the relationship. It, in fact, sets a tone of mistrust and distrust between the parties. When it happens so early in the relationship, this can be difficult to overcome.

It is understandable and quite appropriate for a potential partner to have a certain healthy reluctance to share very personal information such as age, height and weight with strangers, however. Similar to the money issue, there are some positive ways to handle this, without violating trust or your own values and beliefs.

Look again at the example of an appropriate response to such an issue which was included in the Sample Profile in Appendix D. With a bit of humor, and the reassurance of a recent photograph, the uncomfortable moment is alleviated with grace and honesty. And by a recent photo, we are talking about one taken within the past year.

Another positive response would be to see this information provided in a height or weight range or by use of a descriptive comment, such as "Rubenesque," in response to the appearance questions. This type of comment is sufficient to give you, the reader of the profile, a general idea of her appearance or his size, without an exact number, which can feel like a personal violation at this stage of contact. Again, a general idea of body style or appearance is really the information you want. Most daters, online or otherwise, truly don't care about a potential partner's exact height or weight anyway.

For example, if you are interested in a partner with a waiflike or svelte appearance, you don't have to have an exact weight to figure out if the profile you are looking at belongs to someone you would be interested in getting to know. A description or photo will easily accomplish this intended purpose. For this reason, some evasiveness, chiefly in the form of a general description and a photograph instead of actual numbers, are acceptable in this area.

Age

Age is a bit of a different issue than weight, height and money. It has become a bit less of an issue these days, with our understanding that age is only a number. While you will want to see some response to profile questions about age, so you have some idea of, at least the generation of the person you are communicating with, something general such as an age range can be appropriate and acceptable here as well.

Photos can also be helpful in determining a general category as long as they are recent photos. As with weight, most people are not as interested in the exact number as they are in the general idea.

Additional Caution Signs

There are a number of other causes for concern when communicating with a potential partner online. The key component in deciding whether you should be cautious or concerned about a partner or relationship is your instinct about the communication you are receiving. If it doesn't feel right and doesn't seem right, it probably isn't, at least to some degree. Pay close attention to your gut instinct when communicating online. After all, it can be all you have in some cases, as you don't have the former safeguards of friends in common or a history together of attending the same school or church.

Follow up and reliability are also important. Are you communicating with a person who does what she says she's going to do? If she says she'll respond tonight, does she? If she says she'll send a photo, did she?

Inconsistency in writing style can indicate problems. First, it may indicate that you are communicating with more than one person. Or it may indicate that the individual you are corresponding with has emotional, alcohol or drug problems. Ask yourself if it seems like you are getting a reasonably consistent response from the person you are talking with.

A reluctance to exchange pictures can be a cause for concern. But there can be legitimate reasons for a reluctance to do so. Read over Chapter Four regarding the choice to include a photograph to resolve any concerns regarding this issue.

If your partner only emails late at night and in a cryptic style, that can be a sign he is either married or involved in another long term relationship. If you notice this pattern, investigate the situation with him to satisfy yourself that this is not the case.

Getting too attached too quickly is cause for concern as well. If your partner immediately wants to meet or says "I love you" after just a few messages, be very, very careful. These can indicate a controlling, potentially abusive partner or an individual that is looking for a partner to make her whole, feeling she is an incomplete person when alone.

In either case, the relationship will be destructive. In the latter case, while it may be flattering at first, the partner is likely to be so needy you will be feeling quite overwhelmed before too long. Further, anyone that can profess love after only a few contacts does not know you well enough to love you and, in most cases, has no idea what real love is. Run away!

Evaluating the Photograph

You will also want to pay close attention to the photograph the dater includes. This can be an illuminating experience for several reasons. Your potential partner has made some choices in determining which photograph to include that can give you valuable information about his personality. There are some questions you will want to think about:

♡ What Does It Tell You About The Individual?

The first question you will want to ask yourself is what the photo tells you about the judgment of the person who sent it. Look back at the example of the profile at the beginning of this chapter. Note the description of the photo sent: a dirty and torn T-shirt, uncombed hair, cigarette in his mouth.

What you want to ask when you observe these things is whether the values exhibited here are in accordance with your own. If you are a person who takes meticulous care in her appearance, as my client is, it quickly becomes apparent that this person may not be a good fit for you. In fact, I would not hesitate to say that this woman is probably my best dressed client. Her clothes are probably not the most expensive, but she pays meticulous attention to detail, accessorizing each outfit thoughtfully and appropriately. This man would drive her crazy with his careless appearance.

What about the judgment of a person who would choose to include a photo of himself in an unclean shirt and with a cigarette in his mouth to make a first impression on a potential love interest? What are the values here? They did not seem consistent with hers. If she were a smoker and less meticulous about her appearance, perhaps.

But why use a photo like this to make a first impression? Because it wasn't very important to him? Would the new partner or the relationship be important to him? Or would she be treated just as carelessly?

This may be a meticulous analysis of the photograph, but I do this to raise some questions that I would like you to think about as you evaluate and examine photos you are sent or come in contact with on dating sites. Always ask yourself what the picture can tell you about the individual who chose it. Then sit silently and wait for your intuition to kick in and provide some feedback.

♡ Would You Take It Home To Mother?

Another wonderful way to evaluate a photo of a potential partner is to question whether you would take the photo home to mother. Or to show to other important family members? Or to close friends or co-workers.

If not, why not? Would you be embarrassed to show the photo or the individual to persons who are important to you? What does that say about the photo? About the individual in it? About you? About the people who are important to you?

Keep thinking about these questions as you continue to evaluate the profiles and photographs you find on the dating sites. Who would you be comfortable bringing home to mother? And why? This will help you to evaluate whether the profile you are reading is likely to bring you in contact with someone you could be happy with, or with someone you would be frustrated attempting to change. Make your choices accordingly.

A Caveat

Now that I've given you an entire chapter of advice on evaluating a profile and a photograph to choose a partner who is similar to yourself, you may also want to take a look inside and ask yourself if there are some things about yourself that you may want to change. If you are very focused on appearance, perhaps a partner with less of a focus on looks could be a challenging learning experience. If you are very attentive to detail, perhaps a match that focuses more on the "big picture" and less on the minutiae of everyday life could broaden your horizons. If you are very focused on the trappings of modern society, such as clocks, calendars and punctuality, perhaps a partner who is more comfortable away from a day planner could help you become more flexible.

If you are consciously choosing a partner to explore other ways of being, be prepared to be a bit uncomfortable. Let the other person know, early in the relationship, what you are up to. These relationships can provide us with some of our greatest learning experiences, as well as instilling an appreciation and respect for persons different than ourselves, but they definitely take us out of our comfort zone. At times, we may not be at our best when faced with or challenged by ideas and values very different from our own. Make sure your match knows what he is in for and is up to the challenge. If you don't, and he stumbles blindly into this kind of a situation, you could end up just causing both of you a great deal of misery and unhappiness.

As a therapist, I do think this is a valid and valuable approach to seeking a partner. I believe it is healthy to understand and appreciate other ways of being; I think that enables us to be kinder, gentler and more respectful persons.

But I also believe that a potential partner has the right to know if you are choosing to make this type of a change so she can choose whether to put herself in this situation. I can tell you from my work with couples that, as much as this kind of thing can add to a relationship and make it more interesting, it can also add a level of conflict that can be disruptive and painful in addition to the regular work of relating intimately to another human being. Be open with what you are looking for so you know you have a partner who is up to the challenge, or at least willing to explore it with you.

In concluding this chapter on evaluating dating profiles on the web, please look over the summary provided on the following page for a quick review. Don't forget to read over the sample profiles in Appendices C, D and E for examples of what you are looking for and what to avoid. Good luck!

"What You Don't Know" Summary

♡ **There are a number of common "red flags" or warning signs that tend to appear in a profile:**
~Negative comments about others
~Discussion of former partners or past relationships
~Arrogance
~Troublesome references to childhood or family
~Focus on alcohol or drug use
~Dissimilar interests or hobbies can be a problem
~The "children" issue

♡ **Be wary of evasiveness, especially regarding:**
~Work
~Living Arrangements or Marital Status
~Children
~Money

♡ **Use care when evaluating personal statistics and age.**

♡ **Additional caution signs:**
~Pay attention to gut instinct
~Lack of follow-up, reliability or consistency
~Reluctance to exchange photos
~Emailing only late at night
~Getting too attached too quickly

♡ **Use care when evaluating a photograph:**
~What does it tell you about the individual?
~Would you take it home to mother?

*"Honesty is the first chapter
of the book of wisdom."*

~Thomas Jefferson

Chapter 6

"The Rules"

Computer Dating Etiquette

"**A**nd then he sent me this," finishes Sally, clearly indignant as she hands me an email from a man she met online and whom she had seen twice in person.

I read, "While I really have enjoyed our time together, I need to tell you that I met someone with whom I want to have an exclusive relationship. I wish you all the best."

Knowing that Sally had experienced several other online dating relationships in which the men had simply disappeared after several dates, never even emailing her again, I am impressed. This was clearly an improvement!

"Well, it was nice of him to share that with you," I respond positively, "And in such a nice way."

"No!" Sally exclaims, "It wasn't! You don't break up with someone in an email when you've met in person and exchanged telephone numbers. You should call or see them in person. It's online dating etiquette!"

Yes, even in online dating there are rules of etiquette that must be adhered to. Just as for many aspects of other relationships, there are accepted ways to contact and respond to others to maintain the dignity and privacy of each person. Becoming aware of these expectations can keep you from breaking them and unintentionally offending someone.

In the session described above, I had been impressed with the gentleness and sensitivity shown by the man who was indicating the lack of interest. Especially in light of the fact that the last two persons this particular client had dated had gone out with her several times, then dropped off the face of the earth, refusing to even respond to follow-up email she had sent. To me, this was definitely an improvement. But not to her! It was not how things are done. I didn't know enough to be offended. She did.

Making Contact

Prevent yourself from unintentionally offending someone. Read through this chapter on proper etiquette and take it to heart. You can only benefit from treating others with respect and following the rules of engagement.

The Wink

Many sites have cute and characteristic ways to let someone with a posted profile know you would like to communicate with them. On the Match site, and several others, it is customary to "wink" at someone you would like to talk to. It is how you let them know you are interested. The ball is then in their court to respond if they so choose.

As we discussed in Chapter Two, when registering on a site, take time to read through the instructions so you learn what the procedure is for indicating interest and, also, to learn what to look for from a potential partner. Most sites are quite user-friendly, especially the larger, more widely known sites, so even the computer novice should be able to learn to navigate them quite easily. Again, use the options at your disposal to maximize the return on your investment.

The Response

As soon as your profile is listed online, you may be contacted by potential dates. You will want to check your mailbox regularly so that you can respond promptly when you are winked at or contacted by someone online. There are a couple of simple basic relationship techniques you will want to remember in considering your response.

First of all, be honest. If you are asked a question, give an honest answer. If you are not comfortable answering the question, say so. Be impeccable with your word. Say nothing that is not true. A relationship based on a lie is doomed to either fail or make both of you miserable.

Secondly, be safe. Do not give out any personal information until you are reasonably certain the relationship will continue. Do not share your telephone number or home address or place of employment with a contact until you have spent some time communicating online with this person and have found him trustworthy. You can assess this if he does what he says he will do and his responses seem consistent and genuine.

You will not know this the first time you talk with him, but over time, even email responses take on a pattern of consistency or the lack thereof. Looking them over, you can see or sense that they come from the same person and that that person is probably being honest in his communications with you.

As a therapist, this is an incredibly important, yet easy way, to help guide my clients in their contacts with partners. If they can bring me a series of email communications, I can help them look for indications of consistency and point out any patterns of behavior and communication that don't seem to add up.

Gut reaction is important here. Attend to it and do not share information that could hurt you to give out until you feel you know the person and can trust him with the information.

Do not use your main home email address for your dating email. Set up another account to be used strictly for your online dating. This protects your billing, bank account and other important information from being confused or contaminated with or by the dating account. It is also easier to keep the different parts of your life separate in this manner, i.e. work vs. play.

Ask and Answer Questions

There is no such thing as a stupid question. Ask as many questions as you are inquisitive about. Satisfy your curiosity about this person. All of this information helps you to get to know her. It's part of what makes the relationship happen. Think of questions as the tools to help you learn about each other.

To that end, you will also want to answer all questions you are comfortable answering as honestly and completely as possible. It may be, too, that while you are initially uncomfortable answering a particular question, as you continue to have contact you will become more comfortable sharing additional information about yourself. Take it upon yourself, then, to add any information you would like to in order to clarify a previous response.

If You're Not Interested

If you are contacted by someone online and you have no interest in talking with him, you have a number of choices. One is to provide no response at all. While this would seem impolite when communicating in person, it is actually quite a common and well-accepted response when there is no interest in an online relationship. This is true for several reasons.

Most persons who are contacting potential partners online are not contacting just one person at a time. They may "wink" at or initiate contact with several or several dozen.

In addition, there is little investment required to indicate interest, in terms of both energy and finances. As a result, the loss experienced by not receiving a response is minimal.

The assumption in the event of a lack of response is simply that the contactee met someone else and is engaged in exploring a relationship with that person. Whether or not this is true, there is no reason to take this sort of thing personally. Be patient and keep trying. Eventually you will meet the right person, or more likely, a number of right persons, for you.

You also have the choice to respond when contacted by someone you have no interest in dating. You may say you do not feel you have enough in common or are looking for something other than what they have to offer. It can be kind and helpful to be specific in a situation like this.

It is also customary to wish him well and be generous with positive feedback. This can include adding something to your response such as, "You seem to have many wonderful qualities. I am sure you will find the right person."

Your other choice is to have a standard response that you use when someone does not interest you which may or may not be true. You may be more comfortable indicating that you are involved in an exclusive relationship, even if you are not. Be aware that you pay a price when you are dishonest and may eventually get caught in the lie. As a therapist, and a person who is an advocate of gentle honesty in relationships, I can tell you most people usually make out better and more positively, no matter what the situation, when speaking the truth.

This does not mean being harsh or brutal with the truth, however. You needn't state the truth in a hurtful manner, but can say it kindly and gently. My recommendation, both personally and as a relationship therapist, would always be to look for a gentle way to be honest about what you feel.

Responding to Ads

In addition to having partners "wink at" or indicate an interest in you, you will also be choosing, from the pool of eligible singles on your site, those whom you would like to get to know. Read over the profiles and what they say they are looking for carefully to determine if you would be a good match. Follow the writer's wishes. For example, if the man of your dreams says he is looking for a statuesque brunette and you are a petite blonde, you'd probably be better off not responding. Save yourself the trouble and the heartache of a lifetime of feeling second best.

If he is looking for someone of a specific religion, heritage or background and you do not qualify, move on. Don't waste your time or his. You will most likely be happier and less frustrated with someone else. If you do pursue the relationship, you both may always be wishing that you met the criteria your partner initially specified. Relationships started on this basis seldom result in lasting happiness.

How to Get Started

If you are stumped for what to say and how to start, comment on her profile and pay her a compliment. A response to her profile will tell her you have read it carefully. Further, everyone likes to hear nice things about themselves so finding something nice to say about your prospect can go a long way toward helping you stand out from the crowd.

The one caution I would offer here, however, is to be careful about complimenting her looks or her photo. If the first thing a partner hears from you is, "You have beautiful eyes," or "You have a nice figure," she will wonder if you are only attracted to her appearance. A positive statement about an interest or accomplishment would probably be a better choice. You can always compliment her looks later when she knows you are interested in more than how she looks.

"What else should I include in my response?" you ask. You don't want to write the great American novel and scare him off, but you do want to tell him a little about yourself and why you think the two of you might be compatible. Include a few sentences about you and your interests that he could not already find in your profile and, also, what attracted you to him. Interspersed among these statements you may want to include a few well-placed questions about him. This shows you are curious to know more about him as well.

You will also want to read over your prospect's profile carefully before you respond. If the writer has requested persons responding to answer a particular question, answer it as clearly and completely as you can. Try to reply to an ad with a response that you would enjoy receiving. Have fun with it!

If There is No Response

All online daters have the experience of contacting someone and receiving no response. If this has not happened to you yet, expect it because it will happen. I do not say this to be harsh — it is simply the reality of the experience.

The best way to avoid any and all rejection resulting from responding to an online contact is simply not to participate. Just resign yourself to the fact that some of the matches you contact will respond, but others will not, for a variety of reasons. Do not take this personally. It is not about you.

You will also be contacted by a prospect you have no desire to get to know. Think of it as simply part of the experience. You can't take this personally and should attempt to let it go immediately. It will do you no good to focus on it or let it prevent you from contacting another prospect.

It can be helpful to know that there are some characteristic reasons why people decline to respond to an online contact. First of all, many persons listed on these sites are either officially "out of play" or have recently become involved in a relationship they want to pursue. In addition, some sites include profiles of persons who have never officially "signed up" and paid, but perhaps only initiated a trial membership. These persons are most likely unable to respond when you attempt to contact them and, in most cases, do not ever receive your contact.

Some people receive so many responses that they become overwhelmed and unable to answer them all. This is especially likely if the person you wrote is either newly listed on the site or extremely attractive. In either case, she is likely to be inundated with responses to her profile.

Your prospect may have read your profile and looked at your photo and just not felt any chemistry or connection with you. If you are consistently getting no response, get some additional feedback on your photo and profile to determine if they should be changed. But not everyone you contact will feel a connection with you and that's OK. You are looking for **a** partner, not **all** partners.

Another reason prospects don't respond is that the profile contains or reveals an issue they cannot get past; a dealbreaker, as it were. For example, you discuss how you love your cats and he is hopelessly allergic. Or, perhaps there is something about your religious preference or smoking or drinking habits that would prevent a successful or fulfilling relationship, at least from his perspective. Trust me that it truly **is** better and less painful to find this out now, rather than to spend several years making each other miserable before reaching that conclusion.

You simply cannot take the lack of a response personally. You have to go into this game understanding that not everyone you want to talk to will reciprocate. When this happens, you pick yourself up and move on.

In fact, when you contacted this prospect, you most likely responded to one or two others at the same time. Haven't you heard from one of them? That's where you want to focus your time and attention, rather than on feeling sorry for yourself. It's a much better use of your time and energy.

Allow Your Online Relationship to Develop

When you have found someone you want to communicate with and the feeling is mutual, you will want to engage in a series of emails to each other. See Chapter Seven for a more extensive discussion of the process for developing a relationship with a new online partner.

The goal of these continued communiqués is to further your information about this person to determine if you want the relationship to continue. A second goal is to gradually give her some information about you so she can make the same determination on her own. There is a certain etiquette to this process that you will want to be aware of.

Be Patient

Take your time and get to know the person you are corresponding with. Make sure the person you are meeting with has answered all of your questions and given you as much information as you feel you need to choose to continue the relationship. If you are feeling pressured to move to the phone or meet in person too quickly, move on. Do **not** rush into anything. I cannot stress this strongly enough.

Be Honest

We have already discussed honesty at length in Chapters Three and Five regarding profiles so I won't go into detail here. Suffice it to say that if you are not being honest and clear, you are not accomplishing your goal of sharing information about yourself. You may find yourself communicating online with a prospect who is crazy about you and wants to develop a relationship, but he may know nothing about who you really are. What chance does your relationship stand? In all honesty, very little.

Keep It Short

While you want to learn about him and share information about yourself, be careful not to overwhelm a potential partner with too much information too quickly. Further, if it takes him twenty minutes to plod through the three page email you sent, you may find him avoiding your responses in favor of those that are easier and faster to read.

The most successful clients and prospects I see usually keep their emails to a paragraph or two. They can be read quickly and responded to, without a lifetime commitment in terms of attention span. Refer back to Chapter Three, under the heading of **"Too Much of a Good Thing,"** for a discussion on the ease or difficulty of retaining extensive information. It will most likely be more effective, if you have much to share, to do it a bit at a time, rather than in one massive tome.

Questions to Ask

What is important for one person to know may not matter to another. Most people want to know that the person they are dating is not married or committed to another. This is an important question to ask outright if it is not automatically shared in the profile or other subsequent contacts, especially if there are indications that another partner may be in the wings. Indicators tend to be vague responses regarding these questions, only late night communications and unavailability for extensive periods of time.

For another person, it may be important to know that you share the same political or religious beliefs, lifestyle choices, such as vegetarianism, or a strong commitment pets or to an exercise program. Think carefully about your lifestyle and what is most important to you. This information should direct the questions you find it important to ask of potential partners.

Using open ended questions is a good technique for learning much about someone. When you ask a question he cannot simply provide a one word answer to, you get information about what he chooses to include, as well as his attitudes, beliefs, values, state of mind, grammar, phrasing and the like. You can often learn a lot about someone by asking a few open ended questions.

When you are asking questions in emails, start with those most important to you. When faced with several questions in one message, it is easy to get caught up answering the first one read and forget to respond to the next. Remember, this is where you will need to be persistent and come back to ask again. You want to increase your chances of getting a response by putting the most important issue first in your message.

It can be a reassuring technique to offer something personal about yourself when the question you are asking is for personal information. For example, starting out with, "I find I have more time on my hands now that my daughter's away at college," can be a nice way to lead up to, "How old is your son?"

These may seem like simple things but they can make or break a budding relationship. You can save yourself much misery and frustration by asking the important questions up front and then having the courage to face the answers.

Pay Close Attention to the Responses You Get

When you ask a question of an online acquaintance, pay close attention to the response you receive. Some people might not lie outright, but may deceive you by omitting important information. For example, a contact may hide the fact that she is not really single, but has a partner or is, in fact, still married. Ask these questions and if you get a vague or indirect answer, ask them again. If the response is still not clear, move on.

As we discussed in Chapter Five, pay attention to your gut reaction to what you are reading and, later, when you graduate to telephone contact, hearing. If you have a sense that something isn't right, you are most likely on target. At the very least, the issue bears further investigation. Ask more questions to see if she can eliminate your concern.

Save Hot Topics for Later

You will want to save some of the more sensitive subjects for after your first few emails to each other have cleared. After all, if the two of you have nothing in common and little to talk about what does it matter how she voted in the last election or what church he belongs to?

Politics and religion are two areas that can be pretty hot to handle via email. You may just want to save these issues to be discussed on the telephone or in person once your relationship progresses to those later stages. Or to be broached via email once you are certain there is a potential relationship in the making.

Words to Use

We have all heard the expression "You catch more flies with honey than with vinegar." In relationships, a little sugar goes a long way. When you have something to say or a question to ask, the more positively and gently you can state it, the more positive the response is likely to be.

Anyone can understand the need to ask questions and gather information as a way of getting to know someone, but no one likes to be interrogated. You can ask the same question in a friendly tone, or, perhaps, a more subtle way, as you can in a confrontive, provocative manner. If your potential partner begins to feel like he is being cross-examined, he will most likely shut down and you will no longer be learning anything useful about who he really is.

What outcome are you looking for? If you are looking for the truth at all costs, even if the relationship does not survive, confront your new friend. If, however, you are truly looking to learn a few things about a new friend, sugar is your best choice. This does not mean you should not ask the difficult questions. It simply means you will want to ask them courteously and politely for your best chance of a positive outcome.

Expectations

Be cautious about your expectations in communicating online. For many people, online dating is something they do for entertainment or in their spare time. The business of life, commitments to children, family and work can get in the way of the time she may have available to check email and to respond to you online.

Do not expect an immediate response when you attempt to contact someone. If they are a dabbler in the online dating scene, it may take days, weeks or even months before you get a response. Do not take this personally; just chalk it up to the fact that she has not met you yet and has other demands and obligations on her time.

One other thing you will want to be very cautious about is getting too attached too quickly. The best, healthiest and most successful relationships start and build slowly. Take your time. Do not push too fast or try to have a great deal of contact too quickly. You are likely to scare someone away and also get hurt in the process.

Print Everything Out

When you are communicating with a prospective partner online, it is a good idea to print out the complete profile of that person. For one thing, you can never be sure how long he will continue to be a member of whatever site you discovered him on, or he, you. Once he is off, his profile often disappears, as does your ability to compare it against his emails and telephone conversations with you for the sake of consistency.

In addition, print out all emails you receive from him. Even if you are not discussing them with a therapist, over a period of time, they can give you a pretty comprehensive view of the personality of the person you are dealing with. Whether this turns out to be a good or bad thing, it is good for you to have this information, even if you choose to do nothing about it for the time being.

This can also help you keep people straight. Most online daters are communicating with a number of people at the same time. It can be helpful to have a file or list of each person's likes, dislikes, personal preferences, children, employment, significant life events, past relationships or other important or sensitive issues they may have shared with you.

Finally, they give you the ability to verify the consistency of his responses. This is especially helpful if your gut reaction to this person or his answer to a particular question has sent up a red flag. It may not feel good to learn this information, but it can be extremely helpful. I cannot tell you how many times I have discussed a pattern emerging in emails with a client and, more often that not, these have played out in the course of the relationship.

It is a good idea to print out your own emails and responses as well. It can be very useful to know what aspects of yourself you have shared with whom, especially when it comes to some of the more sensitive issues you will discuss, such as past relationships, medical or financial issues, children or a criminal history.

Ending a Relationship

As you can see from my example at the start of this chapter, there is a complete set of rules of etiquette about the process of ending a relationship. For that reason, we will take a separate section to explore this issue and the right and wrong way to do it.

By Email

When you have concluded that a relationship is not working for you and you no longer wish to invest yourself in it, it is customary and polite to let the other person know this, as gently as possible. If you have only communicated via email, it is appropriate to use email to share this information. You can say something such as, "I am aware that our relationship is not really what I am looking for, so I am going to investigate other options."

You have probably been doing so anyway, but this is a nice way to justify your stopping contact with the person you are not interested in. There are only so many hours in a day and you are indicating that you will be spending your time investigating other possibilities.

Another option is to say something such as, "I have enjoyed our chats, but have met someone that I want to investigate a more serious relationship with so I would like to end our contact for now. I wish you all the best." This can also leave your options open for future contact if you want to maintain this possibility in case you decide, given some time to think it over, to explore this relationship further.

Again, some people, probably those uncomfortable with endings or with conflict (and who isn't?) simply stop responding to online contacts. This is a way of getting the message across, eventually, but believe me when I say that it happens much more quickly if you are honest and upfront about it when you first make that decision.

When you do not respond to email, eventually the writer does "get it" but it truly is easier to receive this information up front than to have to figure it out over a period of several weeks. I've seen a number of clients struggle with this and would <u>always</u> advise the direct approach as being kinder and gentler.

It does not take a lot of courage to send an email; it's not as difficult as actually telling someone in person or even over the telephone. If you're going to break it off, have a heart and do it directly.

If You're Instant Messaging

If your relationship has moved to the Instant Messaging stage, it is appropriate to let her know via an IM communication that you don't feel you are a match. You can say something like, "I'm going to sign off. I've enjoyed getting to know you but I don't think we're a match. Good luck in your search."

If she responds by trying to convince you to continue talking, it is acceptable to simply sign off. If necessary, you can block the person from contacting you further.

It would be inappropriate, however, to just break off a conversation in mid-sentence or even simply saying, "Gotta go," and signing off. You should at least provide an explanation about your intention to break off contact.

If You've Exchanged Telephone Numbers

If you have progressed to talking on the telephone by the time you are wanting to end the relationship, it is considered proper online dating etiquette to share that information on the telephone rather than in an email. I realize it takes more courage to tell someone on the phone than to write an email where you may not have an immediate response, but consider that there is more of an investment in the relationship if you have exchanged phone numbers and listened to each others' voices. There is a greater degree of intimacy, as it were. It is only honorable to respect this by saying out loud the words that will end the relationship.

If You Have Met in Person

In addition, if you have met in person by the time you want to end things, it is most polite to do that in person as well. It does take a greater degree of courage to do so, but again, there is an even greater investment and degree of intimacy in the relationship. You two have actually looked into each others' eyes and observed each others' gestures and body language, so you know more about each other than two people who have just emailed, chatted or spoken on the telephone.

Therefore, while in the example at the beginning of this chapter, my client indicated that, either in person or telephone contact was required to end a relationship that had progressed to physically dating, my rule of thumb would be to use the most intimate form of communication you have had to end the relationship. Do not end it with an email if you have talked by phone and do not end it by phone if you have met physically. Talk in person to end the relationship.

It takes an extra measure of courage to do this in person, but you will feel better about yourself for having handled it in the right and honorable manner. I do not mean to imply, however, that if you have actually slept together (and hopefully you will usually have a pretty good sense that the relationship will work out before moving on to sexual contact) that you tell your partner in bed that you want to end the relationship! Common sense and gentleness are your best guides here.

If there are any other details or matters of etiquette that you are aware of that I have not mentioned in this chapter, please contact me and pass them along. I would like to make this as complete a resource as possible for the online dater and would greatly appreciate your feedback.

Please take a look at the summary on the next page as a way of reviewing the information discussed in this chapter. Take stock of the issues you are unfamiliar with and take some time to read over the sections pertinent to those issues. Then you will be ready to take on the next step in your new relationship!

"You can't choose your circumstances, but you can choose to overcome them."

~Anonymous

"The Rules" Summary

♡   **Making Contact**
~The "Wink"
~Decide whether and how to respond
~Ask and answer questions
~If you're not interested, there is no obligation
    to respond

♡   **Responding to Ads**
~How to get started
~Move slowly; don't rush into a relationship
~Be patient
~Save hot topics for later in the relationship
~Be honest (in what you say and what you
    don't say)
~Choose your words carefully
~Keep it short
~Keep expectations in check
~Questions to ask

♡   **Print Everything Out**
~Each partner's profile
~All emails from each partner
~Your own emails

♡   **Ending a Relationship**
~By email if you're emailing
~By IM, if you're instant messaging
~By telephone, if you've exchanged
    telephone numbers
~In person, if you've met in person

Chapter 7

She <u>Really</u> Likes Me!

Taking It S L O W L Y

"I'm not really dating someone, but I am emailing someone and we're getting to know each other slowly."

"Doug, that's wonderful," I exclaim, excited to hear this news as he had been quite depressed and had sworn off computer dating when a recent partner to whom he had become quite attached had just disappeared, just as his wife of 20 years had done two years before.

"Yeah, she seems really nice," he says, somewhat hesitantly, "And I know she's been really hurt."

"How do you know that?" I inquire of him.

"Well, some of it she told me about and I can just tell from how she responds to me that she's scared. She's not ready to meet yet, or even exchange phone numbers – she's just protecting herself and doesn't want to get hurt again. But that's OK. It's fine with me if we take it slow. I just want her to feel comfortable."

I am thinking it is probably a good idea for Doug, as well, to avoid being hurt again. Apparently we still have some work to do on those past relationships, but I am encouraged by his response to this situation. He, too, is aware of what he needs.

The two areas that I find myself most discussing with clients regarding online dating, and, consequently, most concerned for them about, are evaluating a prospect's profile and following a safe protocol in terms of getting to know a partner. There is a recommended process for the progression of an online relationship, from the first online "wink" or contact to "in person" dating or possibly marriage.

Read over this chapter and get yourself thinking about your own personal protocol for getting to know someone, generally, with whom you will be in a relationship. It is best to have given this some thought and developed some firm ideas about that before getting swept off your feet by Ms. or Mr. Right who is attempting to move the relationship along more quickly than you are comfortable.

Communicating "On-Site"

Your initial contacts with any prospects will be confined to what we call "on-site" communication. This means all of your communication for the initial period of time will take place on and through the dating website you are using.

You will each have independently completed a profile about yourself and submitted it to the site to be posted online. One of you will contact the other through the site and the other, ideally, will respond.

The idea is to remain anonymous throughout this part of the process. No personal information is exchanged, at least initially. You do not know each others' names, addresses, telephone numbers or email addresses. You refer to and contact each other by means of your "handle" or "alias" that we developed in Chapter Three. This is a good reason to make sure your name is one you are comfortable with!

Just about every site has developed a process for continued double blind email communication. This way, you can feel confident that you can chat with someone safely and the only way they will be able to contact you is through your account on the dating site.

Exchanging Email Addresses

Many couples eventually prefer to exchange email addresses that are not provided through the dating website they are using. It can give them greater privacy as well as flexibility in the format of their communications and can be an indication that both are interested in moving the relationship to the next baby step.

Use a Separate Email Address for Online Dating

Think carefully about the decision to exchange email addresses with a new partner. It eliminates the policing of your contacts by the dating site "police" who may monitor the site for inappropriate content. It also implies an added level of interest and intimacy in the relationship. Make sure you are ready to take this step and comfortable doing so.

Be sure, also, to create a separate email account for online dating purposes only. No personal information should be accessible about you by means of this address. Then proceed to use this same address for all of your online dating encounters. Some people develop several different addresses for these purposes, but it can be difficult to keep them all straight and to remember to check each regularly. One separate address for all of your online dating encounters should be sufficient, even if you are very active.

Instant Messaging

Many sites also have instant messaging capability for online communication. For those of you unfamiliar with instant messaging, it is much like an actual telephone conversation in that you are both online at the same time and respond to each other immediately, rather than waiting for an email to be read. The response comes up as soon as it is typed and you can reply immediately as well.

Instant messaging conversations tend to move very quickly and most IM participants are conversing with more than one person at a time. High school students are amazing to watch when engaged in the IM experience. I believe my daughter's record was about 12 conversations at one time. It was so busy it made my head spin. Most adults are probably not capable of this type of speed. Further, in a potential dating relationship, I don't see it as a strength if someone is talking with ten people at a time in the first place. One or two, perhaps. If a potential partner feels he needs to speak with ten people at a time, he may not have the time or interest to devote to a real relationship.

Instant messaging has its own unique form of etiquette, given the speed at which it happens. When you are asked a question, answer it even if the conversation has moved on. You may need to refer several lines back to clarify what it is you are responding to, but it is worthwhile to do so. If you do not respond, the prospect may assume you are being evasive and have something to hide. Take the time to go back and answer the question.

Another unique aspect of IM is the fact that you can do it with ten people at a time. However, if you are not able to do so and respond promptly to those with whom you are conversing, give it up. Imagine having a telephone conversation with someone, but you must wait five or ten minutes for the other party to respond to every statement. How frustrating that would be!

Finally, sign off. When you are leaving a conversation, whether for good, as you feel you have no connection with this prospect, or temporarily and you to plan to talk another time, it is only good manners to say goodbye. After all, you would never just hang up the telephone in the middle of a call, would you? Let your partners know you are signing off.

The One Month Rule of Thumb

You will want to focus on spending a significant amount of time chatting online with a prospect, via email and instant messaging before graduating to the telephone. My recommendation is to communicate only online, either via the site, email or IM, for a period of at least one month. There are several reasons for this seemingly interminable delay.

First of all, email is a wonderful way to get to know someone. People tend to share more personal information and to be more open in their responses when they are not saying things out loud or looking you in the eye. You can learn a substantial amount of information about a prospect, simply by prolonging your email contact. Over time, you will get more specific, detailed and personal information from a prospect online if you can prolong that contact a little longer.

Once they "graduate" to telephone contact, couples seldom revert to online contact again unless they are paying long distance charges for telephone calls. However, with the prevalence of cell phones with unlimited long distance minutes, that may be a non-issue.

The second advantage of prolonging online contact is that, while it does favor the prospect who can write well, it allows every user time to think about his response. Messages can be written and re-written. Thought can be given to reactions. Your recipient can go back and re-read your response. You can deliberate and choose your wording carefully.

As I have stated in previous chapters, emails also make for an effective screening tool. You can print them out and compare them with previous and subsequent emails to verify consistency in responses. Red flags can be easier to notice when reading something for the second or third time. Isn't your life worth this type of careful deliberation?

Email can also be an extremely effective tool to discuss important "deal-breaking" issues such as children, habits and problems. Why even take the time to go to the step of having telephone contact, or, worse yet, meeting in person, if the fact that one of you has a young child living in the home would effectively destroy the other's interest in a long-term relationship? Learn about these important issues early on and with a minimal amount of investment (in terms of energy, emotion, money and time) on both parts. Use email to inquire about children, pets, medical or financial problems, previous relationships, and the like. It is also good to give everyone you converse with the chance to be honest about "little white lies" they may have included in their profile by asking, "Are there any inconsistencies in your profile?" This, obviously, would be easier to inquire online than over the telephone or in person. Finding out now will cut down on the possibility of unpleasant surprises later on.

For all of these reasons, I usually recommend that, absent a good reason to deviate from this schedule, my clients stick to the one month rule of thumb before moving on the telephone contact. I do realize that some people move to the phone much more quickly that that, but it is often with disastrous or less than satisfactory results.

In fact, this past week, a client reported that a prospect gave her his telephone number in the first email contact and, when she called him, tried to set up a personal meeting. That's frightening! If the relationship you're developing is worth having, it's worth taking your time for. If your prospect does not want to wait three to four weeks for telephone contact, perhaps he's not the right prospect for you.

Check Criminal or Legal History

Most states have a website you can access, often free of charge, to determine a resident's criminal or legal history. You can use this to verify information your prospect has provided you with, including his divorce, that speeding ticket he got last year or the law suit resulting from a car accident that he is currently engaged in.

If you also happen to learn that he was charged with Domestic Violence or Theft by Employment, this is good information to be aware of. Even if you must pay a nominal fee to obtain this information, I believe it is worth it.

If you are hesitant to use such an invasive step, I will share a little secret with you. I do this will all of the boys my daughter dates if I haven't known them since Kindergarten. I find that some things are just too important to not take some of these safety precautions. Also, with the availability of these services, I find that most people expect them to be used so are not surprised upon learning that you have done so.

The tools are out there. Use them to your best advantage.

Exchange Photos If They Were Not Posted

It is a good idea, at this point in the relationship, to exchange photos if you have not already done so and they were not posted in your online profile. It is helpful, before you talk with someone on the phone, to have a basic idea of what they look like.

Simply email the photos to each other in one of your regular emails. It is probably best to have a couple of photos to send because, again, that can give someone more of a composite picture of you. But remember, as with photos posted online, each should be in a different setting and different outfit.

Progressing to Telephone Contact

After you have been emailing for approximately four weeks, if you are both comfortable with the idea, it is a good idea to move on to telephone contact. Notice I said "if you are both comfortable with the idea." Some people may not be, such as the woman that Dave, at the beginning of this chapter, was emailing. He seemed to be of the mindset, however, that he would be willing to take things at her pace. My professional opinion in his case was that it would be a good idea for him to take things slowly for himself as well.

How to Make That First Call

Most couples arrange, for reasons of physical safety, for the male partner to give his cell, work or home telephone number to the female partner. He then becomes the party taking all the risk as, even if last names are not shared at this point, a telephone number can be researched in a reverse directory to discover a last name. Further, work phone numbers can be called to reach a voice mail which reveals a last name and even many cell numbers can be traced, thereby eliminating that anonymity.

It is often best to stay relatively anonymous as long as possible or, at least until you feel you have a good sense of the other person's values and beliefs and feel safe revealing personally identifying information to her. While women typically fear for their physical safety, men have reasons to be cautious as well. While perhaps they are not subjected to as much of a physical threat as women (in the course of my practice, however, I have come in contact with some women who I would not want to meet in a dark alley), but there is still the threat of emotional hurt or harm or the possibility that an employment or professional relationship could be damaged (i.e. if she stalks him at work he could lose his job).

Suffice it to say, there are some healthy reasons for caution on both sides. This is another good reason to take time to get to know quite a bit about someone before revealing something as significant as your telephone number.

Basically, the male partner typically provides a telephone number for the woman to use to reach him and, in their last email before the telephone call, the two agree on a time for the call to be made. Ideally, a time limit for the call should also be set at that time. It is better to end the call "wanting more", than to be wondering if the conversation will ever end. A non-threatening way to set this time limit may be to say, "I will have to leave to pick up my daughter at 5:15, but would love to talk around 5:00." The message is clear and positive; the time limit set. This takes the pressure off both of you to have an hour long intimate chat.

Prior to the time for the call, review the profile and emails you have printed out about your prospect. Jot down a few areas for discussion in case your mind goes blank, as is not uncommon, in the middle of the call. In addition, make a list of questions you have that you would like answered. You will not be cross-examining your prospect, but if you run out of things to say, this can give you some ideas. These would include any red flag areas or vague responses you have identified from your prior contacts.

Have your opening line in mind when you make the call, in case you get tongue-tied when he says, "Hello" in that dreamy voice. Write this on the same sheet of paper your list is on, but right at the top, so it is right in front of you when you place the call.

When the time arrives to place the call, either call from a cell phone, which is typically more difficult to trace, or block your telephone number if you do not have this service already added to your line. Have a watch nearby so you can pay attention to the time limit. You will also feel less pressure to keep the conversation going if you know this first contact will only last fifteen minutes. You most likely will not need to set limits in the future, but for this first call, it can relieve a significant amount of pressure.

You will also want to end the call on a positive note. Even if you are not sure you want another contact, assume the positive. You can always change your mind at a later time. However, if you are sure you do not want another contact, you may share that during the call in a polite way, such as by saying something like, *"Well, it seems we don't have as much in common as I initially thought, but it was nice talking with you anyway."*

Jot down notes during your call. When you hang up you are likely to remember little of your conversation. Your notes will help you for the next contact that you have.

Afterwards, send a follow-up "thank you" email. You can also indicate in the email that, although you enjoyed the call and want to talk on the phone again, you don't want to give up your email connection with this person. Remember, email can give you the ability to talk about some of the more difficult issues as they come up and, if your schedules don't completely jive, it may be an easier method of communication for the time being.

What You Can Learn From Telephone Contact

While the emailing aspect of the relationship often ends when telephone contact begins, even though it does not need to, you can gain additional information about your prospect by means of this new form of contact. You can tell much by the tone of voice someone uses when speaking about a particular subject. This will give you a sense of the emotion a potential partner is feeling. An animated voice speaks volumes.

You will also learn if your prospect is able to listen and pay attention, as he will have the opportunity to provide you with immediate feedback. If he seems distracted or provides little in the way of a response to your conversation, this would be cause for concern.

Additionally, you will be able to get a better assessment of his sense of humor. While it is possible to convey a bit of humor via email, it is not an easy thing to do. It is much easier to hear this in a voice than online. And with humor typically listed as such an important aspect of a partner, your relationship can move forward by leaps and bounds if you "click" with regard to this aspect of your personalities.

Finally, the time delay from stimulus to response is removed so you will get a much better idea of how well he thinks on his feet. When emailing, as we said, there was time to deliberate over a response. Now that is removed and the response is instantaneous. Pay attention to whether your reaction to this person is the same as when responses were well-thought-out. Do you find him as attractive now? Do his responses seem consistent with those he gave before? What does this mean to you?

But That's Not How I Thought She Would Sound!

Prepare yourself for the fact that the voice you hear may not match your fantasy of what it would be. When we see a photo of someone and email her, we develop expectations about how she will sound. These impulses are seldom accurate so prepare yourself for this fact and deal with it. Plan to put no weight on the sound of your prospect's voice until you have had several conversations with her.

To give you an idea of how common this is, I once had exactly the opposite experience. When I was in graduate school I had a professional relationship with a woman who had the most wonderful, melodious telephone voice. It was rich and warm and conveyed a level of caring and personal interest that was highly unusual. At the end of my work with her, I had the opportunity to meet this woman face-to-face and I was shocked! Her face was quite unattractive, to the point of being startling when meeting her in person after speaking with her on the phone. It was a good lesson for me and I am sure my surprise showed on my face when we met. I only hope my look did not offend her.

So, when you pick up the phone, brace yourself not to react. Voices are easy enough to get used to when we develop a level of comfort with them. They are typically not deal-breakers for most people.

How Long Do We Have to Do This? The One Month Rule

In looking at how long to wait before meeting in person, I, again, take you back to my one month rule. I recommend to my clients that they spend about one month talking on the phone with this new partner (combined with emailing, if desired) discussing everything from soup to nuts before progressing to a face-to-face meeting.

What they typically find, is that spending all that time talking and getting to know someone before investing in a meeting, they tend to have a higher success rate for the personal meetings as they are better able screen out persons that may not be appropriate for them.

Also, spending two months getting to know someone, can lead to a build-up of anticipation and excitement that makes the first meeting a wonderful experience. Face it, by then you know all about each others' significant life experiences, past relationships, children, interests, dislikes and probably a great deal about her values and beliefs. What a set-up for success!

What to Talk About

Most people feel some concern about the first few telephone contacts with a new person. Others, when faced with the idea of exchanging only telephone and email contact for another month, think of this as a waste of time. I see this as an extremely valuable learning opportunity and the chance to lay a solid foundation for your new relationship. To see it in this light, you will need to think about the goals of your telephone contact.

First and foremost, it is a chance to gather more information about each other. You can share stories about your childhood and school years, in addition to some relationship history information so you have some of the details that are important in assessing whether you will want to take the relationship further. Think before you call of all of the pieces of information you would like to have about this person and make a list before you pick up the phone. Then, when you have moments of silence in your conversation, as you inevitably will, you can take those times to introduce one of the areas you want to learn more about.

Also, take time before you call to go over the profile of your contact. You may want to read over Chapter Five to refresh your memory about some of the potential red flags that can become apparent in a profile. Make a list of any of these areas of concern, because, as we discussed in that chapter, they may not be serious enough to eliminate a partner, but are definitely areas you will want to learn more about. Your month of telephone contact is an ideal time to investigate these red flags before you get any further into a relationship in case there is a "deal-breaker" in the mix.

A second goal of the telephone contact is to develop a feel for the type of person you are getting to know. Is she short and terse in the morning? Is he tense and anxious after work? Is she relaxed and amiable, even when her children are around? How does he handle life's little frustrations, such as being cut-off in traffic or receiving an unexpected bill in the mail?

Your conversations with this person over the next month will give you more of a feel for the kind of person you are dealing with. Then you will be better able to assess whether this is someone you want to know better or whether you would be more comfortable not taking the next step.

Assessing the consistency of her responses and the information she shares with you is another important goal of your telephone contact. This is crucial in terms of both your safety and the development of trust in your relationship.

For example, if she tells you she will call at 5:00 p.m. on Tuesday evening, and you don't hear from her until noon on Thursday, this will help you to assess how much weight you can put on plans made with her. If she has forgotten the plan or simply dismisses the lapse, you will know not to count on her to do as she says. If, however, when she finally calls, she tells you she was in an automobile accident on Tuesday at 4:00, you can decide to give this incident little weight in predicting future behavior.

You may also want to jot down notes during these informational conversations, as you may want to be able to compare what you learn to what has been said at other times. If, for example, he tells you that last Easter he was on vacation in the Bahamas and, a week later, mentions that he spent Easter in Big Sky, Montana, that is something you would want to be able to question.

You would need to be able to check this out to determine whether he was simply confused and referring to two different years or is a chronic liar so you should not put too much weight on anything coming out of his mouth. You would also then want to assess whether this is a relationship you want to proceed with. Notes can be extremely helpful in a situation like this, where you might be tempted to second guess yourself if you had nothing written down ("Maybe I was mistaken," "Maybe I just heard wrong,")

Your note-taking needn't be an extensive or onerous process, however. You can just have a notebook or sheet of paper near you and doodle while you talk. When something that may be significant is mentioned, make a little note of it. Then, when you are second guessing your recollection, you can look at your doodles and notes and see that you did, indeed, write down "Easter—Bahamas." You will then want to take the step of clarifying this comment.

The final important goal of this extended telephone contact is to become comfortable with each other. As you get used to each others' voices and get familiar with your histories, you develop a comfort level that can lay the groundwork for a good relationship and a more relaxed first meeting.

It is still important to pay attention to your gut reaction to your contact at this time. Are you comfortable talking with him? Is she easy to talk to? Do you have a lot to talk about? This can help you assess the relationship as well. Take the time and give your relationship a strong foundation.

Short-Circuiting the Process

I am often asked, typically by those new to online dating, if there are any exceptions to the one month rule. Obviously, there are exceptions to every rule and you must use your best judgment. But before you do so, read over this chapter and the next and give some serious thought to your reasons for rushing to meet this person. Think carefully about what you are hoping to accomplish and why you are wanting to short-circuit the process.

There are a number of more common reasons for wanting to move up the physical meeting. Some people are convinced that if they put off the meeting for another month, whether or not this is being requested by the partner, the match will lose interest. Others feel so lonely or needy that they feel they cannot wait. Still others are wanting to give in to requests or, perhaps demands, of a potential partner to meet more quickly. Finally, some persons are facing life events which they think provide good cause for moving up the meeting. I would like to explore each of these reasons in greater detail.

For those of you afraid of losing a partner if you put off a meeting, I would want to explore where this is coming from. Are you feeling insecure in yourself? Could your confidence use little shoring up? If this is your reasoning, you may want to spend a bit more time working on your self esteem before arranging a meeting. Perhaps you could use the time you would be spending rushing into this relationship to do so.

If you are feeling so lonely that you feel you just cannot wait another month to meet this match, you are truly in no position to be developing a relationship with anyone other than yourself. Get yourself focused on the things that are important to you and put off the meeting until you feel like a whole and complete person in yourself. When it comes to relationships, two halves do not make a whole, regardless of what the church says!

Or is your potential partner pushing you to move faster than you are comfortable with? Might you be pushed into taking other steps before you are ready or sure? If this is occurring, it is important to take more time to talk and email with this person to get to know him better before taking the risk of getting closer.

If your online contact is someone you have access to other information about, it could be safer, though may still not be recommended, to meet before one month of telephone contact has elapsed. One of the reasons for delay is to verify the information you are hearing from her by having the experience of continued and consistent contact with her.

For instance, if you become aware that this person lives in your city and can cleverly figure out who he is, you may become privy to additional information about him, for instance by meeting or knowing a mutual acquaintance who can verify some of the data you have been told. In this case, through independent verification and additional sources, you are learning more about the potential partner more quickly than if your only contact is online. You will be able to more quickly assess his truth and veracity as well as, perhaps, to access additional information he is not yet sharing with you. It can, in these cases, be safe and not harmful to meet sooner that one month after beginning telephone contact.

Think carefully about any life events that may cause you to want to move up this meeting. Make sure they are an appropriate reason and positive in terms of the timing for such a meeting. One client that I work with was about to have major surgery requiring a one week hospital stay. Her online contact, who did live in the same city, offered to come visit her after the surgery as their first meeting.

As someone who has survived several relatively minor, non-life-threatening surgeries, I can tell you that I was in no shape after any of these surgeries to be meeting new people, especially one who may become a significant person in my life. When we are receiving medical treatment, much of our control is, of necessity, taken from us. We put ourselves in the hands of the treatment team and allow them to subject us to almost whatever they deem necessary. Our self-confidence takes a beating in this process and for most of us it is a minimum of several days post-hospital-stay before we are ourselves again.

Don't subject yourself to meeting new people when you are in a weakened and vulnerable condition. Delay the meeting until you are yourself again. Telephone contact at that time could be just what the doctor ordered, however, as you may not have the typical distractions that occur at home or in your "real life" to get in your way. You may, therefore, be able to focus yourself on having a good conversation. It may also provide a needed distraction from your medical woes.

Other life events that may provide a less than favorable impetus for moving up a physical meeting might include when anticipating an important evaluation at work, when in the middle of a difficult challenge on the job or when facing another personal difficulty, such as the illness of a parent or child. Because of the intensity of emotion often involved in situations such as these, it is often better to let the dust settle on these experiences before taking on the task of making a favorable first impression. Arrange your meeting when it can truly be the focus of your attention so you can put your best foot forward.

The bottom line is, when you are tempted to meet physically more quickly than recommended here, or to short-circuit any point in this process, think carefully about why you are wanting to rush things. Ask yourself whether there is more work that needs to be done to lay the groundwork for a positive and safe first meeting and a healthy relationship.

If you are in a situation such as that described above, where you have additional information about a potential partner, it can be a positive and healthy choice. If you are not in such a situation, I would stick to the one month rule and take things slowly.

The summary on the following page can help you to further assess these issues for yourself. Please look it over and make wise and thoughtful choices.

"Have patience with all things,
but chiefly have patience with yourself."

~Saint Francis de Sales

"S/he <u>Really</u> Likes Me!" Summary

♡   **Communicating "On-Site"**

♡   **Exchange Email Addresses**
~Use a separate email address for online dating
~Move on to instant messaging
~Remember the one month rule of thumb

♡   **Check Criminal or Legal History**

♡   **Exchange Photos if They Weren't Posted**

♡   **Progressing to Telephone Contact**
~How to make the first call
~What you can learn from telephone contact
~But that's not how I thought she would sound!
~How long do we have to do this?
  (Re-visiting the one month rule)

♡   **What to Talk About**
~Goals for your telephone contact:
~Learning more about each other
~Getting a feel for who she is
~Assessing the consistency of their responses
~Becoming more comfortable with each other

♡   **Short-Circuiting the Process**~Ask Why?
~Am I afraid of losing her/him?
~Am I being pressured to do so?
~Do I have additional information?
~Is there another appropriate reason? _____
_____
_____

Chapter 8

One Day My Prince(ss) Will Come

What to Do When You've Met Someone
You Want To Meet

"**D**o you remember the guy I told you I've been talking to? The one I met online?" Brenda asks me excitedly as we begin our session.

"The one from up North?" I ask, fairly certain I am right as I have heard quite a lot about this man in the past couple of months.

"Yeah. We're going to meet. Next weekend," she finishes with enthusiasm.

"Where are you going to do that?" I ask her apprehensively, half afraid she is planning to drive up to his small town in northern Wisconsin where she would be alone and vulnerable.

"Well, he's coming down here and we're going to meet just for lunch at Applebee's. I've already told my girlfriend where I'm going and when I'm going to be there and I've asked her to call me on my cell phone 15 minutes into the date in case I need to be rescued. I mean, if *he's a real jerk or I'm already bored to death, I can always manufacture a crisis and make my escape!"*

I am impressed.

After you have been talking on the phone for about four weeks, if you are both comfortable doing so, it can be time to schedule a face to face meeting. As we discussed previously, men and women tend to have different fears about the potentials for this meeting. While women's fears tend to center on the possibilities for physical or sexual danger, men tend to fear past relationship experiences and difficult emotional scenes. Each of these fears is valid and should be respected. Guidelines can be put in place to protect against each of these situations.

Safeguards for the Physical Meeting

There are a number of common sense safeguards that I regularly preach to my clients who are dating online. I have included these suggestions below. If anyone reading this book has another idea that they use in this manner, please pass it along to me and I will share it in the next edition of this work.

"First-Date" Anxiety

It is never comfortable to meet someone in person for the first time. However, all of the homework you have already done will make this much easier. You know a substantial amount about the person you are meeting and should have much to talk about—if not, why bother? This really reduces the anxiety level to about a third or fourth date level; another good reason for putting in that two months talking. Not a bad deal!

The other thing you want to think about, to keep the anxiety low, is not to arrange a meeting at a particularly vulnerable place or time. As we discussed in Chapter Seven, you most likely do not want to schedule your first meeting as he comes to visit you in the hospital after major surgery. If you are set up for an evaluation at work or in a situation that may have the potential to affect you personally or emotionally, you would do best to avoid scheduling the meeting near that place or time. Choose a time for your first meeting when you have no other significant life events occurring.

Her Home Territory

In most cases, due to the fears for her physical safety, it makes sense for a couple to agree to meet in the woman's home territory. Notice, I said "home territory" not in her home. If you live in separate cities, you should ideally meet in the city of her residence at a place of her choosing or recommendation. Remember, you are trying to reassure her and enhance her sense of physical safety.

If they live in different cities, some couples discuss meeting halfway or somewhere between their two residences. While this is certainly a good and acceptable idea later in the relationship, many women will have much difficultly and not a little anxiety going along with this. As her therapist, I would recommend against it. Her attention in this meeting is not going to be on her companion, but on her escape route and her safety. In most cases, her home city is your best bet.

Meet in a Public Place

This may seem rather obvious, but when you get to her city or town, you will want to meet in a well-lighted public place. A restaurant or coffee shop are two of the most common options. Ideally, you should schedule this first meeting during the daytime, during a weekday or on a weekend, again for an added measure of safety. Since you are in her town, why not plead ignorance and let her choose the place?

You will meet at the restaurant or coffee shop, both arriving separately and in your own cars. It feels unsafe for many women to jump into a car with a man they have just met. Do not expect this. You each arrive alone and leave alone. If you want to continue the date and go to another location after lunch or coffee, each of you should drive separately, at least this first time.

In making the decision, consider time frame. A lunch date will typically last at least an hour while a coffee date should probably last a half hour or less. In terms of cost and time frame, I usually recommend to my clients that the coffee shop is a better choice for the first face to face meeting. You can always stay longer next time. Remember, just like the phone call, leave them (and yourself) wanting more!

Plan How You Will Recognize Each Other

Remember what we said about the photos you found on the website? They may not be an exact representation of the person you are going to meet. For this reason, and also to reduce anxiety about the whole, "Will I recognize him?" issue, plan a strategy for how you will recognize each other.

Some clever ideas are, obviously, describing the clothing or color you will be wearing or stating you will be carrying an item, such as book of poems, if you can pull that off, or flowers. If you choose the flowers, go with daisies or carnations; roses are too intimate this early in the relationship.

As we said, be aware that your date may look very different from the photo posted on site. If this occurs for you, it is appropriate to mention this gently. In cases of extreme disparity, if you feel strongly about this, it is also acceptable to end the date. After all, how can you trust someone that cannot be honest even at the beginning of a relationship? The tougher times, and issues, are yet to come!

However, most people will usually stick it out for the first date, to gather more information and because, in most cases, it will be emotionally easier than leaving abruptly. Unless there is a great explanation, great disparity between photos and personal appearance that is not mentioned prior to the face to face meeting does raise the issue of trust. Therefore, even if you find that you do enjoy this person's company, you will want to discuss honesty and trust early in this relationship.

Take Your Cell Phone

I would be willing to stick my neck out and speculate that a cell phone is perhaps the best anxiety-reducer for a first date, for several reasons. For one thing, if you are stuck in traffic on the way there, you can call and let your companion know you will be late. Second, if you are in danger (because you haven't followed the above guidelines!) you can call **911**.

Third, if the date is a dud, you can take the cell phone to the restroom, call a friend and have her call the coffee shop to rescue you. This may not be as much of an issue in a coffee date, as they are typically only a half hour or so, but if you get into a lunch or dinner date that can linger, it can seem interminable.

Bring Money

Even if the other party offers and expects to pay, bring money "just in case." Many couples decide to each pay their own way on the first date. Also, you may decide to go on to another activity and want to offer to pay or, at least, contribute to the cost.

On the other hand, if the date is a bust or you are in danger, you may need money to get home safely. Remember, mother always said it's better to be safe than sorry. This advice still holds, even though mom may never have heard of cyber-dating!

Make Sure Someone Knows Where You Are

When you arrange this first meeting, both parties should let at least one other person know where they are, when they will be there and who they are with. In the event something untoward happens, this information could prove invaluable.

Online dating is safe as long as you take care to exercise precautions. It is the people who cavalierly wander off with strangers, telling no one where they will be that show up on the evening news. Don't be a statistic! Be smart!

Have a Friend Call You

Another technique that I recommend to clients is to have a friend call you on your cell phone 15 minutes into the start of the date. If it is only a half hour in length, you may not need to be rescued, but if it is longer, you may want an escape. Hopefully this will not be the case because have done your homework and are reasonably certain you will have enough to talk about for the length of time you will be together.

Regardless of the length of the date, I always recommend that my clients do this for the first meeting. But I would be lying if I told you here that my clients always follow my advice. I can only assume my readers will be the same. If you meet too soon and set up a three hour "date" with someone you barely know, you may truly need to be rescued.

For a variety of reasons, others may need this as well. It is not a bad idea to have a friend call at a specified time. You can choose to respond with something like, *"I'm having coffee with an interesting young woman,"* meaning *"I'm fine,"* or *"Oh no! I'll be right there!"* if you are feeling the need for an escape.

Like the Telephone Call, End on a High Note!

Again, it's best to end before you want to. Leave them wanting more, so you have something to look forward to. Even if you are not certain how you feel at this point, it is best to leave the door open for future contact. It is never a good idea to burn your bridges prematurely, whether with a job or a relationship. Even if you are feeling that you may not want to pursue the relationship further, given time to reflect on the date, you may change your mind.

If, however, the date was a bust and you both know it, you may want to say something right away. Perhaps you discovered a deal-breaker, such as political or religious beliefs that you cannot live with, or you get into serious conflict while having coffee. Saying something now could save you the trouble of having to do it later.

In any case, if there is any abusive behavior that occurs, do whatever you have to, to get yourself out of the situation immediately. Take your cell phone to the restroom and call a friend or *"911"*. Do not continue the date so as to not make waves.

Follow Up with an Email

It is polite to send a follow up email thanking your prospect for her time, the coffee or whatever you can think of to thank her for. This is only good manners and, even if you are not sure you want to continue the relationship, it is a good idea.

Evaluating the Date

Well, now you've done it! Perhaps you're frustrated that it took so long to finally meet. Perhaps you're glad you tried it my way.

Whatever your reaction, you are now either on your way to your first online romance or have your first trial run under your belt. Spend some time alone after the date evaluating your reaction to it. It is helpful to think over the conversation you had and the things you learned. You are doing this not to second guess your own conversation, but to evaluate the response of your partner. You may also want to jot some notes in your notebook so you will recall any new information later.

The most important thing to tune into is your gut-reaction to the event. Are you happy and excited? Do you look forward to seeing her again? Did there seem to be some chemistry between you? Did you feel safe with him? What else do you want her to know about you? How can you imagine sharing your interests with him? Or, are you glad the date is over? Did it seem an unusually long time? Is your overall reaction to the date positive or negative? Do you want to see him again? Pay attention to your immediate, gut-level response to these questions.

Continue to Proceed Slowly and With Caution

Having accomplished your first meeting does not give you the green light for rushing the relationship. You will still want to proceed slowly and cautiously. Remember, anything worth having is worth waiting for. Patience is a virtue!

So how are you to proceed? Have no fear. Again, I have a few rules of thumb to pass along to you. Read on!

See No More Than Once a Week for Several Months

Yes, this means one date a week! You will, of course, want to continue to talk on the telephone and, perhaps, email each other more frequently than this, but you do not want to incorporate this person into every aspect of your life.

It is important to keep this relationship somewhat separate from the other major areas of your life until you are sure it will be a long-term significant and meaningful relationship for you. This separation includes your children. This will enable you to focus on the other areas of your life that are important to you and will prevent you from getting too attached too quickly.

Again, Be Cautious of Pressure to Move More Quickly

One of the biggest red flags in a relationship occurs when one partner pressures the other to commit very quickly. Saying, "I love you," on the third date tells you this person either attaches too quickly or has no idea what love is. Probably both. This can be a person who will be very needy and will quickly overwhelm and consume your life.

As a therapist doing both marital therapy and domestic violence treatment, I see many of these types of relationships involving a rush to relationship. One danger is that we can become too involved with a partner with whom we are a poor match. Perhaps you have been looking for a relationship for some time or have been through a painful breakup in the past. Now you meet a partner who tells you you are beautiful and that he wants to see you every day. He loves you, he says, and it feels very good to have this attention, so you give in and agree to a significant amount of contact for which you know you are not ready.

Before you know it, you are living together and, perhaps, planning a wedding. One day you wake up and realize that you really have little in common and are arguing more frequently. You find yourself looking for ways to be away from home when he is there. In the meantime, the wedding invitations have been mailed and all the plans made.

I would be a wealthy woman if I had a dollar for every person who told me they had had serious doubts about their marriage before the wedding, but went ahead because it wasn't "that bad" and they didn't want to make a scene. You want to take a sensible and reasoned approach to this relationship to prevent this kind of thing from happening to you.

Or, perhaps, you are involved with someone who insisted on more contact too quickly. Again, you gave in because you were flattered to find someone so enamored of you as to want to spend every waking moment together. Pretty soon, she doesn't want you to spend any time with your friends or family and becomes resentful of any time you are not together.

You realize she is very controlling, only now you are living together, you have co-mingled your assets and you are in deep enough to make a quick escape impossible and <u>any</u> breakup difficult and complicated. Remember, it is much easier to take a relationship slowly to begin with than it is to go back and slow things down later. It is impossible to unbreak an egg.

Make No Permanent Plans for Six Months

Continuing our quest to take this developing relationship slowly, my recommendation is that you make no permanent plans, such as marriage, living together or buying a house for at least six months. Remember, if you are seeing each other once a week, this will still only give you 25 face to face contacts before making a life changing decision. Looking at it this way, it perhaps even seems too soon.

Six months is generally a good length of time over which to assess a person's character and personality. You will have the opportunity to observe him in a variety of situations, both good and bad, so will be able to assess whether this is someone you want to travel your life path with. Remember, anyone can seem like the perfect partner when things are going well for him. Six months gives us the opportunity to observe his reaction to some of the difficulties life can toss his way and this can be invaluable in the kind of information it can provide about what kind of a life partner he will be.

Delay Introducing Your Children to a New Partner

Clients often ask me when it is OK to introduce children to a new partner. This depends on several factors. First of all, I am assuming you have sufficiently recovered from the ending of any previous relationship and are in a position to be looking for a new partner.

Assess Whether You Are Truly Ready for a Relationship

It will be helpful at this time to read over Chapter Ten of my previous work, *Child-Friendly Divorce: A Divorce(d) Therapist's Guide to Helping Your Children Thrive*. This will provide a more complete discussion of how to assess whether you are in this position than is appropriate to provide in this text. This work assumes that the reader is recovered from past losses and has dealt appropriately with the baggage ensuing from these previous relationships.

A simple rule of thumb is that if your divorce is not yet final, you are most likely in no position to be looking for someone else. This is true **regardless** of what your former spouse or partner is doing! Do **not** make the mistake of using **her** behavior as an indication of whether or not **you** are ready for another serious relationship.

As previously stated, in this book I am assuming that you have already made this adjustment and are ready for a new relationship as that is the focus of this work. If you know you are not there, please take the time to do the work and make the necessary adjustments before even embarking on a new relationship. You will be glad you did!

Determine Whether This Is a Significant Relationship for You

Many persons experiencing a breakup, making the adjustment and now participating in online dating, experiment with what we call transitional relationships. These are relationships in which there is never an intention to participate in a long-term commitment; just a mutual meeting of needs and companionship. There is nothing wrong with this type of a relationship, as long as this is the intention of both parties and you are both open about it. In fact, it is a very healthy way to get back into the dating scene and begin to learn what you do and don't want in a life partner.

Do not even contemplate introducing your children to one of these short term partners. You would just be buying them an additional, entirely preventable loss and additional heartache. Children can become attached to a new partner very quickly, convincing themselves, even if you warn them otherwise, that this person will be their new "mommy" or "daddy." They can be devastated when these relationships whither and die, as they inevitably will.

Protect them from this loss. Keep your children out of these transitional relationships, even if they ask to be a part of them. That kind of request may be an indication that they are not getting enough time or attention from you. You may find that if you spend a little extra time with your children, they will not be so eager to share you with your new love interest and you just may end up with some adult/couple time which you, also, need.

Kids also just want you to be happy. They may think that they can help facilitate a long term relationship, not understanding that you, and the new partner, have already determined that it is not possible or desirable in this relationship. Children understand and process events differently from adults. Our brains are not fully developed until we are 18-25 years of age. The reasoning abilities develop last. As a result, your children will not be able to understand these relationships at the same level you do. Make decisions carefully to protect their fragile emotions and attachments.

Consider the Ages of Your Children

How quickly you involve your children will also, to some extent, depend on their ages. Young children obviously will develop attachments more quickly than older teens or young adults. While you will want to put off introducing a partner to your children until you determine this will be a significant and meaningful relationship for you, you can probably involve older children sooner than younger ones.

Preferably, younger children should not be involved until you are talking about long term plans. Older children can probably tolerate a quick introduction and limited involvement once you are certain the relationship is a significant one. Every situation is different, so you will need to assess your children's likely reaction before any introduction is made. Again, read over Chapter Ten in *Child-Friendly Divorce* for other ideas on making this introduction as well.

Be Cautious About Sexual Contact

In this day and age, with the disease and danger that can be associated with sexual contact, most persons are comfortable being sexually involved with only one person at a time. This is most often a wise choice.

Talk About Sex, Openly and Often

Even before you are ready to engage in sexual behavior with a partner that you are seriously interested in, you will want to be talking about your values and beliefs regarding sex and other important issues. These discussions may arise in emails, telephone calls or in person, or all three, but it is important for any relationship to develop the ability to communicate in some fashion about difficult issues.

While it is initially difficult and uncomfortable to bring up the issue of sex, if you do not do so now, what will happen after you have co-mingled your lives and problems and conflict does arise, as it inevitably will? It is best to practice now and develop the ability to work out amicable and acceptable solutions to both of you. This will be good experience for later issues and problems that you may encounter.

Make Sure You Are Ready for Sexual Contact

These discussions should happen long before actual sexual contact begins. Most persons in this day and age wisely insist on a commitment of exclusivity before any kind of sexual activity takes place. These days this only makes sense.

Even aside from the dangers associated with sexual involvement today, it can be emotionally confusing to be sexually committed to more than one partner. It is often difficult for us to separate our emotions from attraction, so for most people it is easier and healthier to be involved with only one person at this level at a time.

Talk to your partner. You will want to have cleared the hurdles of deciding that this relationship will be an important one for you and have resolved the exclusivity question before taking this leap. You will also want to know your new partner well enough to be able to trust him to be honest with what he is telling you. To know this, you will need to have spent a considerable amount of time talking with him, in person, online and on the phone. Take your time and decide wisely and safely.

Don't Hesitate to Ask for Test Results

It is perfectly acceptable, and often expected, to ask for AIDS and other sexually transmitted disease (STD) test results before committing to a sexual relationship with a new partner. Remember, we are far from the day when most couples were being introduced to each other by family members or meeting at church. Further, most couples have not grown up together and known each other forever as often was the case in the past. That's why people are meeting online, after all.

It is important to be tested if you have had several sexual partners over your lifetime. Further, it is positive and healthy to share those results with a new partner so that she can make an informed choice about her relationship with you; it is also acceptable to ask the same from her. This is a conversation couples need to have today, when they decide they are ready for this step in their relationship.

"Remember that great love and great achievements
involve great risk."

~Anonymous

Take a look at the summary on the next page. Review the concepts covered in this chapter to assess your readiness to arrange a meeting or to move your relationship to the next stage. Understand that the impulse will typically be to rush to move things along faster than is recommended because it feels good to meet and become close with a new partner. Being prepared for these feelings and impulses will help you to make wise and healthy decisions regarding these choices in your life.

Good luck and happy dating! But remember to make SAFE choices!

"Respect yourself
if you would have others respect you."

~Baltasar Gracian

"One Day My Prince(ss) Will Come" Summary

♡   **Set Up Safeguards for Your Physical Meeting**
~Take steps to reduce your anxiety
~Meet in <u>her</u> home territory
~Meet in a public place
~Plan how to recognize each other
~Bring your cell phone along
~Bring extra cash
~Make sure someone knows where you are
~Have a friend call you
~End on a high note!
~Follow up with an email
~Evaluate the date for yourself

♡   **Proceed Slowly and With Caution**
~See no more than once a week
~Be cautious of pressure to move more
   quickly than recommended

♡   **Delay Introducing Your Children to a New Partner**

♡   **Make No Permanent Plans for Six Months**

♡   **When Ready, Talk About Sex Openly and Often**

♡   **Use Caution with Sexual Contact**

♡   **Ask for Test Results**

♡   **Take Things More Slowly Than You Are Tempted To!**

"I learned that courage was not the absence of fear,
but the triumph over it.
The brave man is not one who does not feel afraid,
but he who conquers that fear."

~ Nelson Mandela

Chapter 9

If This Is Monday, You Must Be ...

It's OK to Play the Field

"**W**ell, let's see," *Cindy begins in response to my question about how she has been spending her free time.* "Last Saturday I went to an Art Fair in Green Bay with Jake. We really had a good time. We spent the whole day there. Then on Sunday, Tom took me out to dinner at a really nice restaurant. I've been seeing him almost once a week now. On Wednesday Jeff and I went for a bike ride after work. That was fun, too. You remember him, right? The builder I told you about? And tomorrow night, Steve is taking me to a movie."

Before she discovered online dating, Cindy, a very attractive woman in her early fifties, had a great deal of difficulty finding companions to spend free time with because most of her friends, co-workers and siblings were married. As a result, she either stayed home or attended events alone – a victim of her environment and the limited resources for singles here. The internet, and online dating, has changed her life.

When many of us were dating or in high school, the rule was to date one person at a time and to commit, often very quickly, to a serious, exclusive relationship. For a number of reasons, the rules have changed.

Talking With a Number of Partners Online Is Normal

First of all, more than 50 percent of first marriages are ending in divorce these days and in excess of 60 percent of second marriages do so as well. Persons who have been through this experience one or two times, want to make sure it does not happen again.

Often, this means they want to be very careful before committing to a new relationship too quickly. The best way to do this is to expose yourself to a number of new people so you learn what you do and don't want in a partner and in a relationship. If you are meeting people online, meeting more people is better than less, as you can better assess what you are looking for.

Secondly, we are becoming aware of the dangers and hazards of attaching too quickly. We understand that it is healthier to have a number of contacts and relationships, rather than putting all of our eggs in one basket, so to speak. It prevents attaching too soon and putting too many expectations on one relationship.

Therefore, in high schools, colleges and among singles of all ages, it is the norm to "see" a number of different people and to delay committing to just one until you are more certain the relationship will be a lasting one. Online dating is no exception. It is normal and healthy to be "talking to," both online and on the phone, and dating more than one person at a time.

Finally, this, also, helps pass the time while you are taking things slowly in your relationships. After all, if you are seeing each partner only once a week for the first six months, you have six nights left to be spending with someone else. Don't you want your partner to have gotten that out of his system before committing to you as well?

Expect Your Online Contact to Be Talking With Others

Given all of these factors, it is safe and reasonable to assume that anyone you meet online is probably talking with others as well as yourself. Remember, this is normal and healthy. It does not mean you will not at some point progress to the point of an exclusive relationship; just that you are not there yet.

Do not expect that he is being exclusive, especially early in your relationship and absent a discussion and agreement by the two of you to do so. This way you are less likely to be surprised or disappointed when you find out he is talking with others as well.

Do Not Take This Personally

Tell yourself this is normal and healthy; do not get upset or negative about the relationship if you discover or simply assume your contact is talking with others. As a therapist, the statement I probably say most often to my clients is not to take things personally. This is one of our greatest downfalls as human beings.

We would all do well to remind ourselves that whatever anyone else does and says is a product of her own reality and life experience and, 99.9% of the time, has nothing to do with us. But many of us insist on running around and personalizing everything and making ourselves miserable in the process. Why not choose to look at any situation in a way that makes us happy, or, at least, content?

Let me give you an example that will hopefully make this clearer. You walk into work one morning and brightly say, "Good Morning!" to your co-worker. She barely glances up, perhaps grunts something and walks on by. Most of us would make ourselves miserable, asking questions like, "Is she upset with me?", "Did I do something to make her mad or offend her?" or "I wonder why she's not talking to me."

Most likely your co-worker's reaction has nothing to do with you. Perhaps she had an argument with her husband before she left the house. Maybe she was frustrated trying to get her children off to school. Perhaps she just received some bad news. Maybe she is simply focused on the work you are all there to do in the first place.

There are hundreds of variables that could have affected her response to you. Choosing the variable or option most likely to negatively involve you only serves to make you miserable. Why not choose to make yourself calm and happy instead? Choose not to take her response personally.

The same is true about a partner talking with others online. Why not remind yourself what a good thing it is that he is investigating other relationships so that if and when the two of you commit to each other, he will be sure that is what he wants. Or that now this frees you up to talk with others as well and to respond to all of those other potential partners that are contacting you. See it as a strength, not a detriment, to your budding relationship.

See Others Yourself

To that end, it is good for you to talk with and see others as well. Don't settle down or jump into a new exclusive relationship too quickly; even if it is self-imposed. Even if you are finding yourself drawn or especially attracted to a particular partner, until both of you are at the point of making an exclusive commitment, do not limit yourself to just that person.

Seek out others; respond to others; contact others. This will give you good information about what you are looking for as well. You will also be more certain that you have found what you want at the point you choose to become exclusive.

Be Honest About Seeing Others; Do Not Give Details

Do not feel the need to "confess" that you are seeing others to your contacts online. Assume that this is the case with both of you, absent an agreement to the contrary.

If your contact asks to see or call you when you have plans with another partner, it is acceptable to simply say, "I'm sorry; I have other plans," and to suggest an alternative day or time. You need not confess you are dating someone else.

If you are asked where you were on a particular evening

when you were out with another partner, with a comment such as "I tried to call you last night but got no answer," it is fine to say something such as "I went to a movie with a friend." If you are asked if it was a member of the opposite sex, it is alright to say so. You are doing nothing wrong or deceitful.

If you are asked if you are seeing someone else, it is best to be honest and acknowledge that you are. Remember it is normal and acceptable. Even if you were raised in a generation when this was not done, challenge yourself not to feel guilty about this. It is expected by most online partners absent an agreement to be exclusive.

You also need not give details about other partners you are seeing, or about other relationships or dates. Most people will not ask you and do not especially want to know. Most would assume that, absent an exclusive relationship, you are seeing or talking with others and that it is none of their business. They would be correct.

Respect other partners' rights to not be discussed or dissected in the context of another relationship with another date. Any potential partner should respect and appreciate your unwillingness to discuss others with them and achieve some trust and comfort from this response.

View Asking for This Information as a Red Flag

If you are asked for detailed information about other partners or dates, I would proceed with extreme caution. I would see the request for this information as a red flag that could indicate a problem with jealous or controlling behavior.

Excessive jealousy typically indicates a partner who is not feeling very secure in himself and who may have more work to do, either personally or to recover from damage caused by a past relationship, before he will be able to be a partner in a healthy and respectful relationship. Talk with him about his concerns and assess his willingness to take a look at his jealous tendencies and seek their origin.

In having this discussion with your new partner, pay close attention to whether he appears to be interested in looking at his behavior and, perhaps, making some changes such as seeking some counseling and working on letting go of past hurts, or whether he is defensive and committed to justifying his jealousy. If it is the latter, this could spell much trouble for the relationship. Think about how much of this you are interested in dealing with. It is easier to get out now if your new partner shows no interest in making changes, than after you have two children together.

Know, also, that attitudes and behavior like this don't just go away on their own. Absent some type of intervention, such as counseling, or a concerted effort on <u>his</u> part to change them, they typically escalate and become more difficult to handle. You may want to save yourself the trouble and get out while you still can!

Requesting this kind of information about another partner or relationship could also indicate some extremely controlling tendencies, which also do not bode well for the relationship. This could mean that she will want to know the details of your every move until the end of time and may want to have a significant influence over them. While she may not come right out and try to prohibit any of your actions or activities, she may whine, pout and complain when you want to go out with friends, go hunting or just spend time without her.

Again, check this out with her. How willing is she to let go of her controlling tendencies? How willing are you to put up with them? Proceed very cautiously if you are getting any of these signals. Make sure you know what you are dealing with and how you intend to handle it.

The bottom line is that you should view any request for information about other dates or partners as a red flag for your relationship. You will want to spend some time investigating these issues further with your match before continuing to pursue the relationship.

Do Not Have Sexual Contact During This Stage

This may go without saying, but while you are in this non-exclusive stage of your relationship you do not want to be having sexual contact. Aside from the complications of disease and safety, you want to avoid the emotional complications and expectations that arise when sex enters into a relationship. If you are not ready to be exclusive, you are also not ready to add a sexual component to your relationship.

When You Are Ready, Discuss an Exclusive Relationship

After you have been dating for a period of time, you may be ready for an exclusive relationship. Do not expect that your partner will just assume this and become exclusive, or that he will read your mind and know intuitively what you want. You <u>must</u> raise this issue in conversation, either online, in person or on the phone. Check out with your partner whether he is ready for this step and make your own decision accordingly.

By now you should know each other well enough to have a sense about what his response is likely to be, but check it out verbally to be sure. If either of you is not ready to make this step, it is your responsibility to say so. Be honest. Your partner will appreciate this, even if it is not easy to hear. Almost everyone would much prefer an honest response to deceit and deception. You can always take this step at a later point in time. Not being ready does not mean that it will never happen or that anything about your relationship needs to change. Some people just prefer to move toward closeness more slowly than others. You can just continue as you have been, dating this partner and others, and see if and how your feelings continue to develop.

The decision to move to an exclusive relationship would probably be an appropriate point to introduce your children to your new partner. To commit to exclusivity you are indeed saying that this is a significant relationship for you. Refer back to Chapter Eight for other considerations in introducing children to a new partner.

As you have done with previous chapters, take a look at the summary on the following page to review the key concepts presented. Read over the example at the beginning of this chapter as well. There is nothing inappropriate about this kind of a social life. Indeed it is a wonderful way to get a secure sense of the kind of partner you are looking for. Variety is the spice of life, until you are ready to be exclusive! Enjoy!

"Talk not of wasted affection;
affection never was wasted."

~Henry Wadsworth Longfellow

"If This is Monday..." Summary

♡ **Talking with a Number of Partners Online is Normal**

~Expect your online contact to be talking with others
~Do not take this personally
~See and talk with others yourself

♡ **If Asked, Be Honest About Seeing Others, but Do Not Give Details.**

♡ **View Asking for Detailed Information About Other Partners as a Red Flag**

♡ **Do Not Have Sexual Contact While You Are in This Stage**

♡ **When You Are Ready, Discuss an Exclusive Relationship**

*"Happiness is a butterfly, which, when pursued,
is always just beyond your grasp,
but which, if you will sit down quietly,
may alight upon you."*

~Nathaniel Hawthorne

Chapter 10

The Only One for Me!

Taking Yourself Out of Circulation

"I *know I'll never be able to trust him again,"* Karla tells me sadly, describing the man she had met online and whose company she had been enjoying for more than six months.

"What happened?" I prompt her.

"Well, I don't know what made me check it out, but it seemed like something I just had to do. He'd come up with another reason he couldn't see me for the whole weekend, so I was home on Friday night, and I went online and checked for his profile and there it was! He had changed his name, but everything read exactly as it had before!"

"And the two of you had discussed having an exclusive relationship?" I inquire, wondering if this could have been a simple misunderstanding, but knowing from the one time I had met John that there had been something about him that I didn't trust as well. I had not shared that feeling with Karla, not wanting to trouble the relationship without something more concrete to go on, but knowing that my gut reaction to people is usually extremely accurate.

"Yes, we decided four months ago that we both wanted to just see each other and we agreed to take our profiles off the site," she exclaims, *"And now I find him still there, but hiding. When I confronted him about it, he just denied it. But it's exactly the same profile he had before. And all of these unexplained absences are starting to add up."*

This example is very similar to a situation that truly happened to a client of mine. She, too, ended her relationship, over an incident such as this. She and her partner seemed to truly enjoy each other's company, regularly going dancing, eating dinners out, seeing movies and traveling together. They got along well and had even taken to spending family time playing games with their children, who also got along very well.

They were in the process of discussing, among other plans, such as holidays and travel, sharing living quarters. They were planning to all move into his home, as it was large enough to house them all comfortably, and, as they lived in different cities, had begun making arrangements to transfer her children to a school in his district. This was not a relationship to be taken likely.

My client shared with me that, periodically, often on weekends, her partner would be unavailable to her and would respond a bit testily when she asked where he had been. Left alone one Friday evening, she was wasting time on the computer and happened to check out the site upon which they had met. Low and behold she found his exact profile, though with a slightly different call name.

When she called and confronted him about this, he maintained his denial throughout the conversation. She knew, however, by paying attention to her instincts, her gut reaction, that she could not trust him. She ended the relationship immediately.

This situation caused both my client and her family extreme difficulty. She had been divorced nearly two years and now had yet another relationship loss to mourn. They had made plans together and she had set her hopes on making them happen. Her children were affected as well. They had started emotionally preparing themselves to change schools and had become attached to their mother's partner and his children.

All parties here suffered several difficult losses that they would not have had, had he been honest about not being ready to be exclusive in the relationship. The attachments would not have deepened and the relationship may, in all reality, have continued, due to his honesty.

No doubt he was dishonest because he didn't want to disappoint my client. What happened was far worse. He broke her heart. It will take a long time for my "Karla" to trust again.

Making the Exclusive Decision

Before deciding to become exclusive with one partner, you will want to give the matter a considerable amount of thought. Think carefully about whether you are willing to forego contacts with all other potential romantic partners in favor of only having contact with this person. Can he or she meet enough of your needs to compensate for the loss of opportunity you will experience by limiting yourself to just one person?

While this sounds quite cold and calculated, actually, when the feelings and chemistry are there, it does not seem like a sacrifice at all, but an opportunity. If you are looking at this like a business arrangement, you are most likely not ready to be exclusive with this person. If you find that what you are giving up does not seem to matter, it is probably the right decision for you and one which you need to be making to give yourself the greatest possibility for a happy relationship.

How to Decide

There are a number of things you can do to help yourself to make this decision. First of all, you may want to review all of your contacts with this partner. Review his profile and all of his emails, as well as all notes you have jotted in your notebook or doodle sheets from telephone calls. This will give you a feel for the entirety of the relationship.

You may want to explore the idea of talking this issue over with a neutral party. Getting into therapy can be a helpful way to process some of these issues. Often, having a neutral third party to bounce ideas off of and to act as a reality check can help you become aware of patterns and behaviors that may have been hindering you for a long time and, certainly, have played a part in other relationships.

Talk to your potential partner about your wishes and hopes, your feelings and dreams for the relationship and your future. If there are any lingering questions you have about this person and your feelings for him, satisfy them now or decline to make your relationship exclusive for the time being. It can be helpful to ask yourself what would satisfy any doubt and whether it is reasonable to expect this from a partner.

Work Through Any Remaining Individual Issues First

You may discover that what is holding you back is an individual issue that you need to work on; that it is not about your partner at all. An example of this might be a fear caused by your last two partners have been unfaithful and leading to an inability to trust. Or perhaps it is that the most important man in your life, your father, left you at an early age, leading to a fear of abandonment from which you have some work to do to recover. Whatever the issue is, if it is a relationship or partner issue, talk to him about it.

If it is an individual issue, take the steps necessary to resolve it yourself before you make a commitment. This may entail some deep thinking or hard work on your part, such as getting into therapy or doing some serious journaling, meditation or introspection to work it out. Again, it is worth taking the time to resolve. You will be glad you did.

Taking Yourself Out of Circulation

If you do decide to pursue an exclusive relationship with one partner, you will want to take the steps necessary to remove yourself from circulation. There is a process to doing this; it involves more than just not going on-site or not checking your email.

If your exclusive partner sees you still in circulation, it can lead to a mistrust similar to what happened to Karla. It can look like you are still keeping your options open. Remember, it is easy to check to see if someone has been active or online recently (i.e. currently or within the last 24 hours) on most sites. If you find your partner still looking, what does that say about your relationship? How secure or committed will you feel?

Remove Your Profile from the Site

The first step you will want to take will be to remove your profile from active participation on the site. This means it will not appear to persons looking for partners on the site, so you will not be getting contacted by any other potential dates or partners.

This should not be a problem if you have committed to the exclusivity of this relationship of your own free will. It will present more of a problem for you if you have simply gone along with your partner's request for exclusivity so as not to disappoint him, rather than because of any desire to do so.

You will most likely need to check with the website to learn the procedure for removing your profile from the site. Some may require you to close your account entirely. Others may allow you to simply remove your profile and keep your account open. You can then decide which option to choose.

And remember, even if you change your alias or call name, if your profile essentially remains the same, or substantially similar to the past, your partner will find you if she checks the site. When I asked Karla what made her look for that profile to begin with, she said that, in spite of the fun they had together, she just had the sense that he was not being honest with her. Again, her instincts proved to be on target.

Contact Others with Whom You Have Been in Contact

If you have had regular contact with a number of other partners, as most people do, it would be appropriate to let them know that you have decided to become involved in an exclusive relationship.

Remember the guidelines we identified to determine how to let someone know this kind of thing. If you have only emailed, email is acceptable; if you have telephoned, give her a call; and if you have met in person, you should really talk to her in person to break the news. It is usually most caring and respectful to use the most personal form of contact you have had to share this information with a partner.

Most contacts will truly appreciate being informed about your new relationship, rather than just having you drop off the face of the earth. I have worked with too many clients who have just been abandoned by former contacts to recommend this course of action to anyone.

Believe me, it takes much longer to move on and to trust someone else when you have no real closure on a relationship. Just not hearing from you keeps her looking, hoping and checking every day in case you have finally contacted her.

Do her a caring favor; let her know what you are up to. You don't have to burn any bridges; if you say it in a caring fashion, most will welcome additional contact in case the new relationship doesn't work out. Consider something like the following:

> *"I have enjoyed our emails and contacts, but I am*
> *exploring an exclusive relationship with another*
> *partner and feel like I need to give it a chance.*
> *Wishing you all the best.*   Sam"*

How offended would you be receiving this message from Sam? Probably not at all. How would you feel if you heard from Sam in several months that the relationship did not work out? Probably pretty receptive. (But pay close attention to the reasons presented for why things didn't work.) Would you be interested in resuming contact? Most persons would be, unless you were exploring an exclusive relationship yourself. Who can blame someone for trying?

Other Reasons to Take Yourself Out of Circulation

Cindy, at the beginning of Chapter Nine represents another good reason for taking yourself out of circulation. As we started that session, she confessed, "Frankly, I'm exhausted! I just can't keep doing this!" In her early 50's and working full time, she found she was having a hard time functioning with such an active social life; exactly the opposite problem than she used to have!

Together, as we talked about her activities, we came to the conclusion that since she had a number of people she regularly enjoyed spending time with, and did not even have time for those, she would remove her profile from the site for the time being. She was simply not interested in meeting new people at this point. She was not ready to become exclusive with any of the men she was seeing; most she had known only 3-4 months. But nor was she interested or able to fit in time for any others. Happy and content, she removed her profile from the website.

Be Honest

The most important aspect of this issue is honesty. Be honest, as well, about your feelings and readiness for an exclusive relationship. Be honest as well about taking yourself out of circulation. Dishonesty in either form is difficult, though not impossible, for a relationship to recover from. Why take the chance? Tell it like it is and fewer people will get hurt.

Take a few minutes to look over the summary on the following page to review the concepts presented in this chapter. Good luck!

"The Only One for Me!" Summary

♡   **Make the Exclusive Decision Carefully**
~Review profile and all email and notes
~Talk it over with a neutral party
~Work through any individual issues first
~Make your own decision
~Talk with your partner

♡   **Take Yourself Out of Circulation**
~Remove your profile from the site
~Contact others with whom you've been
   in contact

♡   **Other Reasons to Take Yourself Out of
Circulation**

~I'm just too busy
~I just need a break from this

♡   **Be Honest**

*"Our attitude toward life
determines life's attitude toward us."*

~Earl Nightingale

Conclusion

And They Lived Happily Ever After!

Summary and Conclusion

"I *just can't believe this is happening for me!"* exclaims Ginny, a *tall redhead in her mid-fifties who has been a widow now for ten years, and who seems almost giddy with excitement.*

"So what do the two of you have planned?" I ask her.

"Well, John and I have been seeing each other, on and offline, for about two years now. I still have five years until I can retire and his clientele is over in Minnesota, so he can't just up and leave. So we've decided to see each other about once a month or so until I can relocate after retirement."

"Then you'll move to Minnesota?" I prompt her.

"That's right," she continues, "I'm going to sell my house and go live with him. By then, my kids will be on their own and with the retirement money I'll be getting, John will be able to reduce his hours so we'll have time to do all the things we enjoy doing together, like sailing, golfing and just enjoying each other's company. Until then, we'll email and talk on the phone when we can't be together."

Ginny's story is truly an example of what can happen when you open yourself up to the possibilities of online dating. As you can see from her comments, she took precautions and let the relationship proceed very slowly, with very positive results. I would hazard a guess that this is the kind of result every one of my online dating clients, and most of you out there interested in meeting a partner online, would hope for. It <u>does</u> happen. I have a number of clients who have achieved this result. You can as well.

The most important caveat is to be safe. I worry about my clients online, which is what prompted me to start preaching at them in the first place about some common sense safety measures. I also kept myself open to learning from clients, both the positive and the negative, about what was possible. Many of the techniques I pass along to you have been inspired by their wisdom. Brenda, at the beginning of Chapter Eight, was truly an inspiration and I can credit her with many of the suggestions I adopted or modified with regard to that first-time meeting.

Brenda went on to develop a significant and meaningful relationship with her date. The last I spoke with her, they were spending romantic weekends together at his cabin in the north woods of Wisconsin. There was a bit of difficulty in that they lived three hours apart and were unable, for a number of reasons, to move closer to each other, at least for the time being. But they were, for now, content to see each other several weekends a month and "talk" via email and telephone during the week, when both were largely too busy to date anyway.

Please heed my cautions to proceed slowly and carefully. I believe that people are basically good, but bad apples turn up everywhere. They can collect in somewhat anonymous locations, such as the internet. Taking your time, asking the right questions, checking legal background and comparing information for the sake of consistency are some of your best tools for uncovering those persons out there who would take advantage of you. Don't be tempted to forego any of these steps, especially if pressured to do so by a partner. Take it slowly. Anything worth having is worth waiting for.

Have fun with this. While most people suffer some anxiety over writing their profile and anticipating the first phone call or first meeting, enjoy the process. Being too serious about the dating process takes the fun out of it. This should be a distraction that may lead to a serious relationship, not a serious distraction. Use humor, laugh and, most of all, be yourself. Don't hide who you are to attract that perfect person. I can promise that if you pretend to be someone you're not, you will be unhappy. You want to find someone you can be yourself with, not someone with whom you will have to pretend to be someone else. If, instead, you find the latter, I can promise you will both be miserable.

I can also offer you a few happy endings to look forward to:

Cindy, from Chapter Nine is currently seeing three very different men she met online. She is also exploring the idea of moving to an exclusive relationship with Jake, who writes poetry for her and with whom she spends at least one evening every weekend.

Dave, from the Introduction, has gotten back on the bicycle and met several women he shares company with. While he is not in an exclusive relationship as yet, he is never lacking for companionship. His greatest lack right now may be his free time.

Debbie, from Chapter Five, had been seeing a number of men she met online, but has currently removed her profile as she was too busy. Also, she wanted to focus more time and attention on an as-yet non-exclusive relationship with Terry, whom she recently met, who owns a lakeside home in a town an hour away. She recently spent a (non-sexual) weekend with him at his home and on his seven beautiful wooded acres and reports that she had a wonderful time.

Doug, from Chapter Seven, is still slowly pursuing the new relationship described at the beginning of that chapter. The two have now met in person and are keeping company on a regular basis. While they have not discussed an exclusive relationship and he has not removed his profile, he has chosen not to contact or see any other partners for the past month.

Jane, from Chapter Three has recently completed her profile and posted it online. At our session this week, she brought in four profiles of potential partners for us to look at and had appropriately identified red flags in three of the four. She was contemplating "winking" at the fourth.

Mary, from Chapter One, recently met a professional widower from her hometown and is in the early stages of exploring this developing relationship. A widow herself, they are finding that they have much to talk about and many experiences to share. Her children are also supportive of her furthering this relationship.

These results are not unusual. There are many lonely people out there looking or hoping for a partner. All you need to do is gather your courage, put a few thoughts together and practice some simple safety techniques.

A positive attitude helps as well. You have nothing to lose by looking on the bright side and seeing the possibilities here, and everything to lose by not taking the chance. Even if a relationship doesn't work out, it usually gives you some information to learn from. You may discover what you are or are not looking for in a partner; or you may become aware of some changes you want to make in yourself regarding how you relate to others.

All in all, you have everything to gain by taking this risk. At worst, you do not find a relationship, but will most likely meet some new people in the process. At best, you may find the love of your life and go on to develop a positive healthy relationship due to the smart choices you have made.

As we said, this is not rocket science. What are you waiting for?

I have to share with you what a pleasure it has been to write this book to share this information with you. I have been accused of being a "Pollyanna" in my work with people and being unrealistically positive in my approach to therapy and problem solving. I see this as a strength, not a weakness, and would always express a preference for seeing and focusing on the possibilities, rather than the potential detriments of any course of action.

Remember your greatest tool is your positive attitude. Nurturing the hope that springs inside each of us that we will find that significant other to connect with can only serve to encourage you to act in ways to make that more likely to happen. If you don't put yourself out there, you won't connect with anyone online. To that end, the best thing you can do is to list your profile as soon as you can, change it as often as you wish, reach out to any potential partners that strike your fancy, respond to those that contact you and be open to the wonderful possibilities that exist. You are limited only by your imagination and your time.

And that same positive attitude is very attractive to potential partners. No one wants to talk to a grouch. The more upbeat and positive you can be, the more likely you are to create that positive and fulfilling relationship for yourself.

I would love to hear your happy endings as well. Please contact me with your stories, either by mail or email and let me know if I can include your story in the next edition of this work. If you've discovered some stumbling blocks that you think others should be aware of, let me know about those as well and I will pass the information along.

Happy Hunting!

*"Experience is not what happens to you;
it is what you do with what happens to you."*

~Aldous Huxley

Appendix A ~ Feedback Form

In my continuing effort to provide accurate, up-to-date material, I would appreciate it if you would take a few minutes to complete the following feedback form. This will help me update and improve the material presented in future editions of this work. Your assistance and time are greatly appreciated!

1. Please rate the following on a scale of 1 to 5, with 1 = poor and 5 = excellent:

a. Content presented	1	2	3	4	5
b. Examples used	1	2	3	4	5
c. Techniques suggested	1	2	3	4	5
d. Chapter summaries	1	2	3	4	5
e. Resources provided	1	2	3	4	5
f. Appendices	1	2	3	4	5

2. What is your overall reaction to the book?

3. What did you most enjoy or find helpful?

4. Do you have suggestions or ideas to be included in further editions of this book?

5. Do you have suggestions for other topics that would be of interest to you?

6. How did you learn about this book?

OPTIONAL: Please add my name to your mailing list to receive information about future books:
Name: _____
Address: _____
_____

Please send the completed Feedback Form to:
Blue Waters Publications, LLC
P. O. Box 411-F   or   *Fax to:* (920) 683-9624
Manitowoc, WI 54221-0411

Appendix B ~ Contact Page

Please feel free to contact the author and publisher in the following manner:

By US Mail:
>Diane M. Berry
>Blue Waters Publications, LLC
>P. O. Box 411
>Manitowoc, WI 54221-0411

By Fax:
>(920) 683-9624

By Telephone:
>(920) 683-3963

By E-Mail:
>bluewaterspublications@lakefield.net

Please also check out our websites:
>www.bluewaterspublications.com
>*(for books and other materials available for sale)*

>www.bluewatersfc.com
>*(the clinic – Blue Waters Family Counseling, S. C.)*

Appendix C ~ Sample Profile

Dancing Queen

Do Ya Wanna Dance?

I love to dance the night away or sail the ocean blue.

Friends say I have lots of energy and I've been described as determined when in pursuit of a goal. I like to ride horses on mountain trails, run, bike or just sit and watch the sun set.

I can be social, but tend to prefer being with just one person. I also enjoy spending time alone, writing, in a log cabin in the woods, and have a little bit of a wild streak.

I am looking for honesty, gentleness and a sense of adventure.

Dance with Me?

Appendix D ~ Sample Profile—With Red Flags

As each dating site has a different format for its profile, I include here some questions and areas of inquiry that may or may not be included in the profile you are using. The point is in learning how to evaluate the responses given in some of the more important and common areas of a person's life or relationship history. In the event your site does not include the questions in this profile, you can always inquire about these areas in your chats or emails with a potential partner. Their responses regarding these issues can be truly revealing. Further, a number of sites simply have multiple choice questions, especially devoted to this area. It is important to inquire further to get more than a pre-selected answer to these issues.

♡**How would you describe your childhood?** Dysfunctional.

This clearly indicates some unfinished business with regard to the past. Ideally, an individual would be able to make some neutral or positive comment, even if their childhood was difficult. See Appendix D for a better response to this question.

♡**How would you describe your relationship with your family of origin?** They're all losers. We haven't spoken for 15 years.

Several big red flags in this response, but this actually appeared on one of my client's potential partner's profile. First of all, it clearly indicates unfinished childhood business. Secondly, the judgment with which he labeled his family members is a cause for concern. An individual who would respond in this manner is likely to say similarly negative things about you when the two of you disagree on an issue. Finally, handling conflict by breaking off contact is typically not a positive situation. You want to remain open to healing the relationship and unfinished business. Remember, relationships are works in progress. This gentleman has closed the door on those closest to him. What does this portend of his potential as an intimate partner?

♡**Do you have or want children?** Never; are you kidding?

This response obviously indicates an extremely negative view of children. If you already have children, or see some in your future, think carefully about this person. Even if your children are adults and do not live with you, s/he is likely to see any contact or need they have of time from you as a threat and an unreasonable demand.

♡**Have you ever been married?** Yes, thank God that's over.

A response like this usually indicates unfinished business related the past relationship(s). Ideally a person will have something more positive to say in response to this question, or simply respond "yes" or "no."

If the individual is over 30, you will want to know if they have ever been involved in a long term relationship. This can give you valuable information about a potential partner. If they have not, ask why not? Seek more information about probably answers. If they respond that they just haven't met the right person, are they too picky? If they say they have been too busy establishing a career to focus on personal relationships, do they have time now for a relationship? If it is because of their parents' lousy relationship, do they have some work to do with a counselor or therapist to work through these experiences?

♡**Are you currently married?** Not really.

This can mean, "I am still married, but thinking of leaving him/her if I meet the right person." A bad idea on all counts!

♡**What is your idea of the perfect date?** An intimate dinner for two at my (or your) home.

Be careful. This can mean, "I expect to have sex on the first date."

♡**What is your employment history?** I've had a variety of different jobs over the years.

This can mean I can't keep a job so I must find a new one every year.

♡**What is your income?** It varies.

Read this as, "I lose my job or get laid off a lot."

♡**Do you smoke or use alcohol?** I like to party with friends.

You will want to be very careful here as well. This can mean "I spend every weekend in the bars." Few people who have problems with alcohol or drugs will actually include that in their profile, if they even admit it to themselves. You may want to include a statement in your profile, such as, "If you are into drugs of any kind or drink more than socially, please do not respond to me." While this may seem extreme, it may save both of you much heartache and frustration.

Notice, also, the smoking question was not answered. This may mean s/he smokes two packs a day and just isn't ready to share that with you as yet. Or it may mean nothing. But you will want to inquire further.

♡**Personal specifics — Height, weight, age, etc.** Unanswered or non-specific answers.

Be aware that many people fudge a bit on these specific pieces of information. Men often add an inch or two to their height, women often drop 5-10 pounds from their weight and many people subtract a few years from their age. While you want to stay away from getting too hung up on finding a man who is exactly 6 feet tall or a woman who weighs less than 140 pounds, as these are only external characteristics, what this area does give you an indicator of is the individual's truth and veracity as a partner. If they are not honest about these basic details, will they be honest and forthcoming about other, more important issues in the relationship? This can therefore be a gauge of their truthfulness as a significant partner.

To that end, while in response to most questions vagueness is not a positive quality, in response to these types of questions, it can be preferable to an outright lie. If you are uncomfortable sending your numbers over the internet, a positive response would be to send a photo and make a general statement that you would prefer to stay away from numbers as they do not define the most important qualities of a person.

But then you must be consistent and not expect your partner to give you specifics either.

♡Anything that makes you uncomfortable.

As we mature to adulthood, we train ourselves to ignore that little voice inside that causes a twinge of concern in response to a person we meet. This is our intuition or our "gut reaction" and an extremely valuable resource in assessing our reaction to a new person. When you feel a twinge in response to a profile response, it is something to pay attention to. This may not be the person for you or you may want to inquire further about whatever it is that is causing you concern.

Appendix E ~ Sample Profile—No Red Flags

This is a profile in the same basic format as Appendix C with healthier, more positive responses. This is what you are looking for, whereas the responses in Appendix C should cause some concern and, at the very least, lead to further inquiry.

♡**How would you describe your childhood?**

It was good. My folks didn't have a lot of money but they did the best they could.

This is someone who either got what he needed physically and emotionally or who has made peace with and accepted the less positive aspects of his childhood. Let's face it, who didn't have something to come to terms with?

♡**How would you describe your relationship with your family of origin?**

We don't get to see each other as much as we would like, but try to get together around holidays and keep in touch via phone and email every week or so.

Clearly there are family connections that are important to this person and he makes an effort at maintaining them. He is likely to put similar effort into your relationship.

♡**Do you have or want children?**

I have two grown children who I love to spend time with when they can make the time to visit.

This leaves the impression that the children are important to the individual, but not the entire focus of her life at this point. She makes them a priority, but the children also are busy, successful and involved in establishing their own lives, independent of their parent.

♡Have you ever been married?

I was married for ten years, but went through a divorce five years ago when my wife left me for another man after we had drifted apart.

This individual does not express undue bitterness about the divorce, accepts some responsibility for his role in the breakup and has had enough time to get some emotional distance from the marriage. All good signs.

♡Are you currently married?

No. I was involved in a two year relationship, but that ended about a year ago.

Again, the individual is not committed elsewhere, has had experience in a long term relationship and has had some time to heal from the breakup. You will eventually want to inquire about how and why the relationship ended, but you have enough to go on to continue having contact with this potential partner for now.

♡What is your idea of the perfect date?

This is very individual and dependent on personal taste. A typical example might be:
Dinner at a romantic restaurant followed by a walk on the beach to watch the sunset.

What you want to watch for is anything too suggestive or sexual (especially in a profile or early contact), overt focus on alcohol and involvement with too many other people. These can all be red flags and portend disappointment or trouble.

♡What is your employment history?

I worked at XYZ company for ten years after I got out of school. Then, when it was sold, the new company ABC, hired me on and I'm still there.

This is a person who is clearly valued and respected as an employee and has a wonderful work history. While there are many reasons for changing jobs, inquire into these and be on the lookout for a pattern of job hopping. It can portend difficulty committing to one employer, especially when times get tough. This can be true of the individual's relationships as well.

♡What is your income?

A good response here is either a number (especially if it's truthful) or a reason why there is no number, such as, "I make a sufficient income to meet my needs and many of my wants, but would like to avoid stating a number, or hearing one from you, because I do not believe that a person with a higher income should be valued more in terms of partnership potential."

This is an honest and acceptable reason for not including a number and the bottom line is, all you really need to know is whether the person can support himself and pay his bills. He has given you that information in a very positive and respectful manner. Some persons believe it is preferable to avoid using a number to respond to this question for the very reason he provides.

♡Do you smoke or use alcohol?

I do not smoke and I drink a glass of wine occasionally. However, I can party without alcohol.

The writer has given you some valuable information about her habits here, sharing that, while she is not averse to occasional alcohol use, it is not an essential part of a social engagement.

♡Personal specifics — Height, weight, age, etc.

While I have no objection to providing this information at a later date, and have included a recent photograph of myself, I believe that a person is more than the sum of his parts so would prefer not to give specific numbers at this point. Suffice it to say I am over the age of consent.

Another appropriate response would be to provide an age or weight range or descriptive comment, such as "Rubenesque" in response to appearance questions. These comments give the reader a general idea, without an exact number, which can feel like a personal violation at this stage of contact. Most people expect and are prepared to give numbers with respect to age, but may object with regard to height and weight. Ranges can also be helpful. Again, isn't that the information you want; most people don't really care about a potential partner's **exact** *height or weight anyway.*

Appendix F—Reading List— Relationship Guides

♡*Divorce Busting,* by Michele Weiner-Davis, MSW,
(Simon & Schuster, 1992)

♡*The DNA of Relationships,* by Gary Smalley, M.D.
(Tyndale House Publishers, 2004)

♡*Getting the Love You Want,* by Harville Hendrix, Ph.D.
(Henry Holt & Company, 1988)

♡*How to Be An Adult in Relationships: The Five Keys to
Mindful Loving,* by David Richo
(Shambhala, 2002)

♡*How to Write a Love Letter: Putting What's in Your Heart on
Paper,* by Barrie Dolnick & Donald Baach
(Harmony, 2001)

♡*How to Write Love Letters,* by Michelle Lovric
(Chicago Review Press, 2004)

♡*Long Distance Relationships: The Complete Guide,*
by Gregory Guldner (Jf Milne Productions, 2003)

♡*Love Between Equals: How Peer Marriage Really Works,*
by Pepper Schwartz, Ph.D (Touchstone, 1995)

♡*Mars & Venus on a Date: A Guide for Navigating the 5 Steps
of Dating to Create a Loving and Lasting Relationship,*
by John Gray (Perennial Currents, 1999)

♡*Mars & Venue Starting Over: A Practical Guide for Finding
Love Again After a Painful Breakup, Divorce or the Loss
of a Loved One,* by John Gray (Perennial, 2002)

♡*Passionate Marriage: Love, Sex and Intimacy in Emotionally Committed Relationships*, by David Schnarch (Owl Books, 1998)

♡*Relationship Rescue*, by Phillip C. McGraw (Hyperion, 2001)

♡*The Relationship Rescue Workbook*, by Phillip C. McGraw (Hyperion, 2000)

♡*Romancing the Ordinary*, by Sarah Ban Breathnach (Scribner, 2002)

♡*The Seven Principles for Making Marriage Work*, by John Gottman & Nan Silver (Three Rivers Press, 2000)

♡*Why Marriages Succeed or Fail: And How You Can Make Yours Last*, by John Gottman (Simon & Schuster, 1995)

♡*You Just Don't Understand: Women and Men in Conversation*, by Deborah Tannen, Ph.D. (Ballentine Books, 1991)

Appendix G—Reading List—Guides for Life & Attitude

On Coping with the End of a Relationship:

♡*Child-Friendly Divorce: A Divorce(d) Therapist's Guide to Helping Your Children Thrive!*, by Diane M. Berry, MSW, LCSW, JD (Blue Waters Publications, 2004).

♡*The Divorce Recovery Journal*, by Linda C. Senn & Mary Stuart (Pen Central Press, 1999)

♡*Getting Up, Getting Over, Getting On: A Twelve Step Guide to Divorce Recovery*, by Micki McWade (Champion Press, 1999)

♡*How to Survive the Loss of a Love*, by Melba Colgrove, Ph.D., Harold Bloomfield, M. D. & Peter McWilliams (Prelude Press, 1976, 1991)

♡*ReBuilding When Your Relationship Ends*, by Bruce Fisher (Impact Publishers, 1982)

♡*Spiritual Divorce: Divorce as a Catalyst for An Extraordinary Life*, by Debbie Ford (HarperSanFrancisco, 2002)

On Life and Attitude:

♡*A Man's Journey to Simple Abundance*, by Sarah Ban Breathnach & Michael Segell (Scribner, 2000)

♡*Feeling Good: The New Mood Therapy*, by David D. Burnes, M.D. (Signet Books, 1980)

♡*The Four Agreements*, by Don Miguel Ruiz (Amber-Allen Publishers, 1997)

♡*God On a Harley*, by Joan Brady
(Pocket Books, 1995)

♡*Life Strategies: Dong What Works, Doing What Matters,*
Phillip C. McGraw (Hyperion, 2000)

♡*Simple Abundance: A Daybook of Comfort and Joy,*
by Sarah Ban Breathnach (Warner Books, 1995)

♡*Something More: Excavating Your Authentic Self,*
by Sarah Ban Breathnach (Warner Books, 2000)

On Power, Control and Anger:

♡*The Dance of Anger,* by Harriet Goldhor Lerner, Ph.D
(Harper & Row, 1985)

♡*The Emotionally Abusive Relationship: How to Stop
Being Abused and How to Stop Abusing,* by
Beverly Engel (Wiley, 2003)

♡*The Verbally Abusive Relationship: How to Recognize It
and How to Respond,* by Patricia Even
(Adams Media Corp., 1996)

♡ *When Anger Hurts: Quieting the Storm Within,*
by Matthew McKay, Ph.D, Peter D. Rogers, Ph.D &
Judith McKay, R.N. (New Harbinger Publications, Inc.
1989)

♡*Why Does He Do That? Inside the Minds of Angry and
Controlling Men,* by Lundy Bancroft
(Berkley Publishing Group, 2003)

*"Even a happy life cannot be without
a measure of darkness,
and the word happy would lose its meaning
if it were not balanced by sadness."*

~Carl Jung

Index

*"No one can make you feel inferior
without your consent."*

~Eleanor Roosevelt

Quick Order Form

Postal Orders: Mail completed form and check to:
Blue Waters Publications, LLC
P. O. Box 411
Manitowoc, WI 54221-0411

Email and   Please visit our website at:
Credit Card   www.bluewaterspublications.com
Orders:*
Questions: Telephone: (920)683-3963
Fax: (920)683-9624

Please send me the following books and articles:
I understand I may return any of them for a full refund – for any reason with no questions asked.

___ **Romancing the Web** $13.95
___ **Child-Friendly Divorce** $17.95
___**A Peace of My Mind** $15.95 (available Fall, 2006)
___ **Positively Managing Your Stress** (article) $5.95
___ **Soothing the Self** (article) $3.95

Please send me free information on:
___ Other Books   ___ Seminars   ___ Consulting

Name: _____
Address: _____
City:_____State:_____Zip: _____
Telephone: _____
Email Address: _____

Sales Tax: Please add 5 % for products shipped to Wisconsin addresses.

Shipping: Please add $4.00 for the first book and $2.00 for each additional book or article shipped.* If you wish to pay by credit card, please visit our website (www.bluewaterspublications.com) at which that option is available   Thank you.